STRESSED OUT

13 POWERFUL METHODS TO STOP STRESS, RECOGNIZE TRIGGERS, CURB TOXIC OVERTHINKING, AND MANAGE ANXIETY

MAX SAMPSON

CONTENTS

INTRODUCTION

Sometimes the most productive thing you can do is relax.

— MARK BLACK

There are two kinds of people in this world: Those who live by a *just stop worrying* approach to anxiety and those who actually understand what anxiety is. I'm the latter, and unfortunately, many people advised me to *just be happy* or *stop thinking about it* when I was at my lowest. Now, I don't know about you, but telling someone mid-panic attack to just *stop worrying* is about as useful as telling a crying newborn to just keep quiet when they're actually hungry and in need of a clean diaper. What's shocking is that so many people think that unsolicited advice such as *just smile more* actually works when in reality, it just makes things worse. It's surprising that so many people think that is a good approach to anxiety when more than seven million US citizens currently struggle with it (Anxiety and Depression Association of America, 2021). Surely, if so, many people struggle with anxiety, there must be some helpful advice out there, right?

Well, yes and no. Yes, there is definitely some helpful advice out there, and no, you will also find a lot of useless and frankly insensitive advice. No wonder so many people are too scared to admit that they struggle with anxiety or any other mental disease, for that matter. If only there was a way to cut through the noise and useless just be happy advice. Good news! That's exactly what I'm planning on doing.

One of the biggest reasons people are currently experiencing such high levels of anxiety and stress is because of financial matters (Elizabeth Scott, 2019). Not only do people fear not having enough money and battling the constant bills piling up on the kitchen counter, but they also feel the need to always get more and chase their careers even further. Perhaps you've experienced this lately, feeling as if you have no control over your own life, unable to make any decisions because you're scared that it might interfere with your work schedule. Or perhaps you feel sick with anxiety because of already jam-packed schedules and a never-ending to-do list, yet you still feel unsatisfied at the end of the day?

I get it. I really do. I've been there! I've felt the lack of control and the ever-present anxiety and stress. In fact, anxiety and I go way back! There was a time in my life when anxiety controlled and ultimately destroyed every aspect of my life: my childhood, my marriage, my career, and my friendships. It also killed my happiness, leaving me in what felt like a pit of never-ending darkness.

You see, that's why I know that avoiding anxiety or simply using "be happy" quotes doesn't work. It also means that I do know what actually works in battling anxiety and why it's so incredibly important to get your anxiety under control. This might be a little hard to hear, but it's the truth:

You can't go on with your life and make a success out of it if you spend every waking moment anxiety stricken. It is impossible to experience all this magnificent world has to offer, build healthy relationships, and enjoy your job without confronting your anxiety and finding a way to deal with it.

If that's why you're here, I'm glad that our paths have crossed. My path through anxiety wasn't a straight and narrow one; it was filled with mistakes and obstacles that tripped me up, but you know what? All those obstacles and missteps equipped me with knowledge and valuable tools to battle anxiety, and eventually, I was victorious. I am a 48-year-old divorced father of seven who has made many mistakes in his life but has learned from every single one of them. Most importantly, I am now anxiety-free. Sure, I still experience stress like every other person, but my mind is free from constant, ever-looming darkness and anxiety, and I want to help you achieve that level of freedom as well.

Through this book, I want to help you address your stress and anxiety and provide you with the tools necessary to manage your stress in order for you to live a productive and peaceful life. Throughout this journey, you will

- learn what stress is and identify what is causing your anxiety.
- gain knowledge in understanding your stress.
- discover ways to battle and manage your stress and anxiety.
- recognize your triggers and deal with them.
- emerge equipped to face any stressful situation.

If it sounds like a lot, take a couple of seconds and breathe deeply. Know that you don't have to face this alone; I will be with you every step of the way. Together, we will face your stress and anxiety and find a way for you to live a peaceful life. Does that sound like a plan?

Before we jump right in, I want to encourage you to keep your journal nearby. If you don't have a journal or you've never used one, I highly recommend that you get one as soon as possible. Journaling is one of the most powerful tools you can use to battle stress and anxiety. At the end of each chapter, you will have the opportunity to journal your thoughts and feelings, helping you to process the chapter information and make it practical for your life. It's one thing to have knowledge on a topic; it's quite another to actually implement it practically. Throughout this journey, we will do both.

My goal and hope for this journey is that you will emerge feeling ready to face whatever might come your way. I want to empower you with the strength to say "no" to the things you need to say "no" to and to say "yes" to yourself and your mental health. It's about time you got the attention, care, and love that you deserve. Are you ready to embark on this journey with me? If so, let's get right into it by taking a trip down memory lane.

WRITING THE STRESS AWAY

Before we jump right in, I want you to grab your journal and write down as much or as little as you like, using the following as writing prompts:

- How do I feel about this journey I'm about to embark on, and why?
- What do I hope to get out of this journey?
- Make a promise to yourself that you'll see this journey through and give it your all, no matter your skepticism.

1

TURNING BACK THE PAGES

Close your eyes for a minute. Think about the first time you felt stressed. It might have been a couple of weeks ago, perhaps a few years, or maybe it's been decades. Allow your brain to travel back to old memories of stressful situations as you try to pinpoint the first time you felt stress enter your mind and body. Warning: It might not be a pleasant experience or a fun memory to relive, but it's incredibly important to turn back the pages of your life story and identify where it all started. Perhaps if I tell you about the first time I experienced stress, you'll feel courageous and face your own story.

The first time I experienced stress and anxiety that was above the norm, I was about seven years old. I grew up in a very dysfunctional family where screaming, shouting, and even physical abuse were considered normal. One day after school, I was playing with my ball in the street. We lived in a very small house in the poverty-stricken outskirts of Detroit, Michigan. As I was playing, I heard screaming and then gunshots coming from a few houses away. I saw two men run out of the house, jump into a black car, and drive in my direction. I sprinted into the house and hid under my bed. In fear of that day's events, I left my ball outside. That evening, when my dad got home from work, he saw my ball outside. I got the scolding of my life for not taking care of my stuff. My dad was completely uninterested in hearing my side of the story and didn't care that I spent the whole day hiding under my bed, waiting for my parents to come home. What my dad didn't realize is that at that moment, stress entered my mind and my body, and I spent years anxious about other people, convinced that no one cared or understood my part of the story.

Only after I identified that memory as the cause of my stress and anxiety was I able to deal with it. You see why it's so important to turn back the pages and find the root of your anxiety and stress? Just like with any other weed, if you don't remove the root, it will always grow back. It's the same with stress. That being said, take some time now and write down your first memory of being stressed or anxious. When you're finished, we'll take a closer look at what exactly stress is and how it affects our bodies and our minds.

WHAT EXACTLY IS STRESS

First of all, it's important to realize that stress is completely normal. Stress is a response to a situation that demands a reaction (CAMH, 2018). In fact, stress isn't just normal; it's necessary for survival. Imagine walking in the park when all of a sudden, a giant dog runs up to you, teeth bared, looking ready to rip you to pieces. What do you do? You climb up the first tree you can find and call for help, of course. Say "thank you, stress," because stress just saved your life! Stress demands that your body release brain chemicals that send signals to the rest of your body to react appropriately. Without those stress hormones, the dog would have shredded you to pieces. The hormones released in your body during a stressful situation do a couple of things, like make you sweat, quicken your breath, tense your muscles in preparation to take action, and send you into fight-or-flight mode.

That's why not all stress is considered *bad*. It's quite normal to experience stress if it's in small doses and easily manageable, like that feeling you get when you're running late for an appointment or the night before a test. The problem comes in when that stress prolongs and never gets released. That's when stress becomes *bad* and causes mental and physical problems (CAMH, 2018). Long-term stress can cause problems such as depression, anxiety disorder, substance abuse problems, insomnia, and bodily problems like headaches, gastrointestinal problems, weakened immunity, and high blood pressure (CAMH, 2018). That's why it's extremely important to diagnose stress in order to manage it before it becomes an even bigger problem and health risk.

Diagnosing Stress

Usually, when you're sick, or you think there might be something wrong, you simply go to the doctor, get a test, and get diagnosed. Unfortunately, this is not the case when we're working with stress. That's because it's subjective and not measurable with a test (Cleveland Clinic, 2021). Only you can determine how you feel in certain situations. The key lies in understanding what you're feeling and comparing it to how you're supposed to feel. For example, if you're so stressed that you feel dizzy and nauseous, no one will be able to tell you how you feel, but you will know. But perhaps you've felt this dizziness and nausea so often that it doesn't seem strange anymore. Only if you tell someone how you feel, and they say that it's not normal, will you realize that something is out of the ordinary. That's why healthcare professionals make use of questionnaires and lists of symptoms of severe stress to help you diagnose your stress (Cleveland Clinic, 2021). If you do have stress, a healthcare provider can help you find the right treatment for your symptoms and for the stress itself.

When you're diagnosed with stress, it's not like being diagnosed with the flu. You don't just get some antibiotics and sleep it away. It requires some input from you, and very often, it requires some serious life changes. I'm not telling you this to scare you or to discourage you; rather, I'm telling you this to help you be prepared for the journey ahead. Let's continue by taking a look at some of the most common reasons for stress. Perhaps you can start identifying where your stress is coming from by taking a look at the most common reasons for stress.

COMMON REASONS FOR STRESS

There's no way of denying that we live in a highly stressful world. From work to personal life to pandemics and political wars, it's all stressful and can add to the anxiety that you're feeling. Perhaps you feel stressed about a certain big event coming up, like a performance evaluation at work or a wedding, but oftentimes it is the little things that add up. Alone, they all seem fairly harmless but combined, they can cause a lot of pain and anxiety (Mind, 2017). Certain things cause different people to feel stressed about life, and that's all part of the journey, but here are the ten most common reasons for experiencing stress besides finances.

Not Enough Time

When you are constantly chasing deadlines and trying to balance all the different aspects of your life, it can easily start to feel like you simply don't have enough time to do everything. Unfortunately, we live in a culture that celebrates *the hustle*. But it's often *the hustle* that puts the pressure on you and steals all your time, leaving you anxious and stressed out with no healthy coping mechanisms in place. Sometimes feeling as if you don't have enough time comes down to poor time management, but in other cases, you're simply overloading yourself with things to do (Realbuzz Team, 2018).

Unhealthy Lifestyle

An unhealthy lifestyle is one of the biggest reasons that people experience stress. Whether you have an unhealthy lifestyle due to a lack of time or simply because you are already stressed, either way, it will lead to additional stress in your life (Realbuzz Team, 2018).

Unhealthy lifestyles reduce your ability to cope with everyday stress, which means that stress levels increase daily without a healthy outlet.

Too Much on Your Plate

Taking on too much is another reason why people are feeling stressed and anxious. If you say "yes" to every single thing, you'll be overloaded with work, and the pressure of responsibility will weigh on you. Taking on too much will prevent you from doing your best work, and it will cripple you with responsibility. I know it's hard to say no to certain requests, but it's a necessary tool to learn when you are feeling stressed (Realbuzz Team, 2018).

Conflict

Another big reason for experiencing stress is conflict at work or at home. If a relationship is strained, it puts a lot of tension on the relationship, which can lead to disagreements and increased levels of stress. No one enjoys fighting with colleagues or loved ones, and if you're usually a conflict-avoidant person and you find yourself in conflict with someone, it can be extremely stressful and feel like the end of the world. No matter how used to conflict you might be, it will ultimately contribute to your stress levels (Realbuzz Team, 2018).

Struggling With Acceptance

If you struggle to accept things in your life, you will experience stress about the things that you can't control. Trying to be in control of every aspect of your life is an impossible task, and it will add to your stress levels (Realbuzz Team, 2018). When you are trying to control things that you physically cannot, you are only creating unnecessary stress and wasting your mental energy. When you're consumed by the things you cannot control, you will also struggle to focus on anything else, which adds to your stress levels.

Lack of Rest

Thanks to an unhealthy hustle culture, we've started seeing relaxation and resting as weakness or laziness. As a result, we're constantly on the go, and the few minutes we allow ourselves to rest are filled with guilt and shame. Failing to take time out adds to your stress levels and can lead to burnout and anxiety (Realbuzz Team, 2018). If you fail to rest, you physically never deal with the pent-up stress, causing you to bottle up everything and add stress on top of your stress (on top of your stress!). Taking a break is not just good for you physically but also mentally. You can't just assume that with hard work, your stress will sort itself out. It's important to take time out and prioritize your rest.

Personal Life Issues

One of the biggest reasons that so many people struggle with stress and anxiety is because of personal life issues. Things like injuries and illnesses can add a lot of stress to one's life. Another big personal life issue that causes stress for many people is having trouble with infertility or unplanned pregnancy. Our personal lives are filled with things that can be stressful, and it sometimes just feels like too much. Even experiencing things like crime or witnessing abuse can add a lot of stress and be damaging to one's mental health (Mind, 2017).

Inability to Laugh

As strange as it might sound, failing to see humor in certain situations can add a lot of stress to your life. Being able to laugh in the face of adversity is a stress management tool that is greatly underrated. When you're able to see the humor in things, something can go from being very stressful to just *part of life* very quickly. For example, if you spill coffee on your shirt just before a meeting, it can either cause you to panic or if you laugh about it and solve the problem with a positive attitude, it is a less stressful situation (Realbuzz Team, 2018). Being unable to laugh at anything that goes wrong sets you up for failure because, subconsciously, you are chasing perfection, which is impossible.

Specific Situations

Some stressful situations are unavoidable, and it's very hard to do anything about them to remove the stress, like waiting in the hospital to hear the news about a loved one's surgery or being stuck in traffic when you're late for picking up your kids at school, and you know that they're waiting all by themselves. Specific situations can add a lot of stress to your life, and it can be hard to find solutions for that type of stress (Realbuzz Team, 2018).

Major Life Changes

The final reason why you might be experiencing stress is because of life changes. Big life changes can cause a lot of stress since they change everything that you used to know. It pushes you out of your comfort zone and forces you to adapt. Major life changes include things like moving, changing careers, getting married, going through a divorce, having kids leave the nest, taking care of elderly parents, retiring, etc. The process leading to the change can be just as stressful as going through the actual process (Realbuzz Team, 2018).

SIDE EFFECTS OF STRESS

Stress is often described as feeling anxious or as a feeling of discomfort, but stress is much more than that. In fact, stress can have some very serious side effects. Studies have found that stress may be the cause of various health problems and that it also increases the risk of heart disease and even Alzheimer's (Griffin, 2010). While some of the side effects of stress don't appear serious at first, they can have serious and lasting effects. Many people shrug off stress and see it as *part of life,* and although that is true to some extent, it's still important to look at the seriousness of stress and not underestimate the severity of stress in our lives.

Let's take a look at a couple of side effects that stress can have on your life:

- heart disease
- asthma
- obesity
- diabetes
- headaches
- depression
- gastrointestinal problems
- alzheimer's disease
- accelerated aging
- premature death

As you can see, these are very serious side effects, and that's why it's so important to find ways to manage your stress and deal with it head-on. Over the years, researchers and healthcare professionals have explored various ways of dealing with stress, from medications to finding new hobbies. Specialists found that art therapy is one of the best ways to manage and release stress.

DRAWING TO RELIEVE STRESS

Drawing for five minutes a day can greatly influence your stress levels in a positive way (Elmer, 2022). Not only is drawing flexible and accessible to all, but it's also something that doesn't require a lot of additional resources. If you have a pen and a piece of paper, you can draw the stress away. Drawing is a wonderful way of managing stress because it allows you to be mindful. A study done in 2018 found that students who doodled before an exam were less anxious and more alert during their test (Elmer, 2022). Before you say, "But I'm not an artist," I'm going to cut you off by saying, "It doesn't matter!" The whole point of drawing is to release tension and stress, not to focus on perfection.

Here are seven art therapy ideas that you can use to release some stress in your life:

- **Scribbling**: Grab a piece of paper and your choice of weapon (pen or pencil) and just go for it. Don't think too much about it, and don't try to be perfect. Just scribble. Allow your mind to run free and just create. It can be words, shapes, or squiggles, as long as you put pen to paper and let loose a little.

- **Shapes**: If blindly scribbling isn't for you, start by drawing one shape over and over again. Allow the shapes to work together to create a pattern. This is also known as Tetris Art, and just like in the original Tetris game, you can work with the shapes to create a satisfying result.
- **Drawing Prompts**: If you're looking for a clearer direction, using drawing prompts might be just what you need. Drawing prompts are lines of inspiration, guiding you as to what to draw. How you interpret it is completely up to you, though. Some drawing prompts can be quite vague, like "draw a happy moment," while others might be more direct, like "draw a robot dog eating ice cream."
- **Mandalas**: Mandalas were created by Carl Jung, the founder of analytical psychology (Elmer, 2022). Mandalas are symbols that work together to create a circular, geometric shape. The repetition of the patterns promotes mindfulness, and a study done in 2020 found that mandala drawing can reduce negative

emotions and improve spirituality (Elmer, 2022). Drawing and coloring mandalas is a great method of releasing stress and tension.

- **Sketching**: If you're not interested in shapes, you can always have a go at freehand sketching. Sketching involves tracing images and then shading them by using different pencils. If you want even more creativity, you can always color your sketch once you're done drawing it.
- **Coloring**: Speaking of coloring, having a coloring book is no longer just for kids. In fact, adult coloring books have made quite the comeback, and it's a wonderful way of releasing stress and tension. If you're not interested in thinking up new pictures and you just want to color an already existing picture, you can find adult coloring books for cheap, and some might even include mandalas.
- **Mixing Mediums**: Drawing is such an accessible way of practicing art therapy, but you don't have to stop at pencil and pen. You can mix up your mediums and add paint to your art therapy or even colored markers. If you want something more dimensional, you can also create collages by adding cutting and gluing to your repertoire.

Although stress is very serious and shouldn't be taken lightly, it is also not something that you have to fear. It's not necessary to stress about your stress because we can do something about it. Drawing therapy is just the first step! In this book, I'll introduce you to a whole world of things that you can add to your life to improve your stress levels, but for now, let's take a quick journaling break before we move on to the next chapter.

WRITING THE STRESS AWAY

Take a couple of moments and think about what we've discussed so far. Then, grab your journal and use these journaling prompts to write down how you are currently feeling. Take your time. There is no rush to get through this as quickly as possible. In fact, I want to encourage you to take at least ten minutes to think and write carefully.

1. What is my biggest source of stress?
2. Right now, what do I feel challenged by, and who do I feel supported by?
3. What art therapy can I add to my daily life that will help me get rid of stress?
4. Why would I like to manage my stress better?
5. How do I usually handle my stress?

2

PUTTING OUT THE FLAMES

Have you ever heard of the word *burnout?* Lately, it's a word that's been flying around, especially in the business world. In my opinion, burnout isn't a new concept or even a new experience, and it's about time that we start talking about it more openly. The more modern our world gets, the more our responsibilities seem to get. It's hard to explain burnout to someone who has never experienced it. It's like trying to describe depression to someone who seems to think it's just *feeling down*. Perhaps you've felt burnout in your life before, but you're not even aware of it. You might even be experiencing burnout to some extent right now. It's that feeling of trying to keep your head above water, but the current seems too strong, so you start feeling an aching sense of dread, exhaustion, and anxiety. You're not sure what's wrong because you've been able to keep your head above water in the past, yet now it seems impossible. That's burnout.

According to Melissa Steginus, burnout is the result of burning more fuel than you put in the tank (Sprankles, 2021). In other words, you give too much of yourself and take too little time to recharge and rest.

If you're reading this and thinking, *That's exactly how I'm feeling,* then I've got some good news for you. You're not alone! A study done in 2021 revealed that 52% of employees experienced feelings of burnout (Sprankles, 2021). That's why this chapter is all about putting out the flames of burnout. We'll chat a bit more about what exactly burnout is, the symptoms of burnout, and how you can prevent it from occurring. Remember to keep your journal nearby for jotting down things that stand out to you. I also want to encourage you to keep an open mind as we explore these chapters and uncover our emotions.

WHAT IS BURNOUT?

Burnout is when you are emotionally, physically, and mentally exhausted because of prolonged and excessive stress (Smith et al., 2018). Burnout begins with normal stress, and as the stress continues, it builds up and drains all of your energy. Burnout reduces your productivity, and it saps everything from you.

When explaining burnout, I like using the analogy of a bucket:

Your daily tasks and responsibilities are like a big tank that needs to be filled with water. Your daily effort is the bucket in your hand that you use to carry water. Lastly, your energy and time are in a deep well of water situated far from your tank. Every day, you fill up your bucket, walk with it carefully to the tank, and pour the water from your bucket into the tank. Slowly but surely, the water level in the tank rises as you complete all your daily tasks. You can see the progress you're making at work and at home, and that energizes you. However, if you carry too many buckets of water, the stress will be too much on the bucket, and holes will start to appear. So, you continue, but as you walk, the water drips out, and by the time you get to the tank, you only have half a bucket of water left. The more you continue, the more holes appear, and pretty soon, you arrive at the tank with a completely empty bucket. No matter how hard you try, you can't seem to get any water into the tank. In fact, you can't even fill the bucket while at the well.

That's exactly what burnout is like.

You might wonder, why didn't the person just stop when they noticed the holes? Well, that's the difficult thing with burnout; it's hard to notice the signs when you don't know what to look for. It might just feel like normal stress, or when the first hole appears, you might convince yourself that it's fine because you don't have time to stop now. That's exactly why every person needs to be aware of the signs and symptoms of burnout so that they can stop and fix the bucket as soon as the first hole appears. Let's take a look at the various signs and symptoms of burnout.

SIGNS OF BURNOUT

Just like a leaking bucket, there are many signs that you might be on the road to burnout, but you need to be aware of the fact that the symptoms you are noticing are signs of burnout. Otherwise, you might look for the wrong solution. For example, if you're struggling to get water into the tank, you might think your bucket's handle is the problem and replace it when, in actuality, there is a hole in the side. Perhaps you might even look for a new well since the well must surely be the problem. My friend, you have to take a break and self-reflect on your life in order to recognize the signs of burnout as burnout and not something else. Burnout signs and symptoms show up in three ways: Physical signs, emotional signs, and behavioral signs. Let's take a closer look at each, and as we go through it, I want you to compare it with your own life and write down the symptoms that you are currently experiencing. That doesn't mean that you have burnout, but it might serve as a good reminder to take some time for yourself and fix the holes before it turns into a mess.

Physical Signs

Some of the first signs of burnout will appear physically. Physical signs of burnout include

- constantly feeling fatigued and finding it almost impossible to finish tasks.
- feeling tired and drained, making it difficult to focus on work.
- experiencing apathy and extreme dissatisfaction with your work.
- frequent headaches, migraines, and muscle pain.
- a sudden change in your diet and sleep patterns.

Emotional Signs

Besides the physical signs of burnout, some symptoms will appear emotionally, which are a little harder to pinpoint. Emotional signs of burnout include

- a constant sense of self-doubt and feeling like a failure.
- feeling helpless, trapped, and defeated.
- feeling alone in the world and experiencing a sense of detachment.
- loss of motivation, finding it impossible to get excited about things that used to motivate you.
- increasingly cynical and negative outlook on life.
- decreased satisfaction and a sense of accomplishment.

Behavioral Signs

Behavioral signs of burnout are often the result of trying to find a coping mechanism for the physical and emotional signs of burnout. Behavioral signs are very difficult to identify on your own and often require the loving words of a friend or family member to point them out.

Behavioral signs of burnout include

- stepping down from responsibilities and adopting an *I don't care* attitude.
- isolating yourself completely.
- procrastinating even with small things.
- using food, drugs, and alcohol to cope with life.

- snapping at others and taking out your frustrations on those around you.
- missing work, coming late, or leaving early, no matter the deadlines.

All of the above signs and symptoms aren't always present when you are experiencing burnout. You might only have one in each group. Burnout might also look different in you and me since it's a very personal experience. Stress and burnout aren't the same things, but stress left unattended can evolve into burnout. That's why it's so important to be aware of your stress levels and analyze whether you might be experiencing some symptoms of burnout.

BURNOUT TRIGGERS

Burnout isn't like a rare disease that just appears out of nowhere. The truth is that burnout is triggered by events in your life. You might be experiencing something in your life that is causing a lot of stress. If that stress persists, it can lead to anxiety, depression, and burnout.

Burnout is usually triggered by one of three things:

1. work-related stress
2. lifestyle-related stress

3. personality traits

Work-Related Stress

An example of how work-related stress can lead to burnout is when one of your colleagues quits, and you get handed the added responsibilities until they hire someone new. So, you start working additional hours to make sure everything is up-to-date. As the weeks pass by, it's clear that they're not looking to hire someone new. You bring this up with management and ask for additional compensation since you now have more work, and they tell you that a raise isn't in the budget. You continue to work as hard as possible, so you start compromising by working late and taking work home. The added stress and responsibilities weigh you down and push you to a point where you can barely cope with daily activities. Pretty soon, you have burnout that is triggered by work-related stress.

Lifestyle Related Stress

Your lifestyle might also be a trigger for your burnout. If you're living an unhealthy lifestyle, or perhaps you've isolated yourself for a long period of time, you might start to experience the signs of burnout. An example of a lifestyle-related trigger might be when your elderly parents move in with you, and you have to take care of them 24/7 since they're not in great health. As much as you love your parents, it takes a great toll on you, and eventually, you don't have the time or energy to do anything for yourself. This can lead to burnout due to lifestyle-related stress.

Personality Traits

As weird as it might sound, some personality types are more prone to burnout than others. If you have a Type A personality, you are more likely to experience burnout than others. That doesn't mean that if you have a Type A personality, you will surely have burnout one day; it just means that you have to be more aware of the signs and symptoms (Scott, 2020). A Type A personality is usually more competitive and work-obsessed than other personalities. Studies have shown that even working closely with Type A personalities can cause stress and lead to burnout (Scott, 2020).

It's important to be aware of burnout triggers in order to accurately pinpoint where your burnout or stress is rooted. Being aware of these triggers will also help you prevent burnout in the long run.

HOW TO PREVENT BURNOUT

As serious as burnout is and as scary as it might sound, it is preventable. The earlier you catch your burnout symptoms, the easier it is to do something about them.

The biggest contributor to burnout needs to change in order to prevent burnout from continuing or reoccurring. That's why you need to identify what it is that is triggering your burnout. If it's your job, chances are that you need to change careers or work for someone else instead. However, before you quit your job, there are other strategies that can help you get rid of your burnout (Valcour, 2016). Let's take a look at four proven strategies for recovering from burnout.

Self-Care

It's essential to prioritize your self-care when you experience symptoms of burnout in order to replenish your physical and emotional energy. When you focus on self-care, you take time to see to your own needs. Self-care isn't a selfish act but rather an act of love. Self-care includes activities such as prioritizing sleep, eating balanced meals, journaling, reading, and enjoying nature (Valcour, 2016). Although self-care is something that everyone should do, it's often pushed to the bottom of the to-do list to make time for other things. When you have symptoms of burnout, it's incredibly important to immediately start prioritizing your self-care and take care of your physical, emotional, and spiritual needs.

New Perspective

Recovering from burnout is not as easy as eating a salad and taking a bubble bath. You also need to put in some work and adopt a new perspective. Identify the things that you can change and let go of the things that you can't. If you constantly stress about things that you cannot control, you need to change your perspective and start focusing on the things that you can control. That doesn't mean that you're not allowed to acknowledge your negative emotions. It simply means that you shouldn't wallow in self-pity. Acknowledge your negative emotions and allow yourself to feel every bit of them, but then choose to focus on something else. This isn't an easy step, but once you're able to focus on things other than what is wrong in your life, you'll start to experience freedom from the things you can't control (Valcour, 2016).

Reduce Exposure to Stressors

The next step might require some dramatic changes in your life that not everyone will agree with, and that's okay. If you know what is triggering your burnout, you have to start limiting your exposure to that stressor. Whether it's work stress, lifestyle stress, or a specific personality type, you need to take active steps to remove yourself from that stressor's vicinity. This might mean that you remove yourself from a toxic work environment or that you arrange a meeting with management. Perhaps it requires you to stop isolating yourself and start doing something meaningful with your spare time. No matter the trigger, you have to start limiting your interaction with it if you want to recover from your burnout (Valcour, 2016).

Seek Healthy Connections

The final strategy for burnout prevention is to seek healthy connections. If you're experiencing symptoms of cynicism and inefficacy, having healthy connections is the best way to fight burnout (Valcour, 2016). Healthy connections can come in different shapes and sizes. You can find a healthy connection in a new pet or by finding a life coach. You can also volunteer at a local charity and build meaningful connections that way while doing something good for humanity. Breaking the negative cycle of self-isolation and toxic relationships is an incredibly important step when battling burnout. If you have healthy connections, you are much less likely to experience burnout. If you feel like you might be under a lot of stress, pay extra attention to your friendships and family members.

Although burnout is not exactly the same as stress, the two often go hand-in-hand. Burnout has the tendency to feel insurmountable when you're in the midst of it all, but take heart: It's not the end, and it can get better.

Take one day at a time and choose to focus on getting better. Before we move on to the next chapter, which is all about understanding stress, let's take some time to journal and do a quick burnout assessment.

BURNOUT ASSESSMENT

Questions	Never (1)	Rarely (2)	Sometimes (3)	Often (4)	Always (5)
I feel drained and without any physical or emotional energy.					
When I think about my job, it is negative thoughts.					
I am less sympathetic than I used to be.					
I am easily irritated.					
I feel unappreciated and misunderstood.					
I feel like I have no one to talk to.					
I feel like I'm not living up to my full potential.					
I feel a lot of pressure to succeed.					
I feel unsatisfied with my career.					
I fear that I might have chosen the wrong career path.					
I am frustrated with my personal life.					
I am too tired to care about friends.					
I feel like there is too much on my plate and not enough time to get to everything.					
I feel like I don't have any meaningful hobbies.					
I find it hard to make decisions.					
TOTAL:					

Score Interpretation

- 15–18: No sign of burnout
- 19–32: Little sign of burnout
- 33–49: At the risk of burnout
- 50–59: Severe risk of burnout
- 60–75: Extreme burnout

WRITING THE STRESS AWAY

1. If I look at my life objectively, do I have any symptoms of burnout? Write each symptom down.
2. What triggers my stress and burnout? How can I avoid this trigger going forward?
3. Do I prioritize self-care enough? How can I start implementing self-care today?
4. Who do I consider to be my inner circle and meaningful connections?

3

UNDERSTANDING STRESS

Thanks to fast-paced lifestyles, work demands, family responsibilities, and pressure from the media, most people experience stress daily to the point where they feel overwhelmed and unable to cope. We already discovered that stress was historically good for us and is one of the reasons we survived, but since we don't have to run from lions daily anymore, we're left with feelings of anxiety and overwhelming fear. Numerous times, we don't even realize that we're suffering from stress, or we realize we're stressed but fail to acknowledge that we need to do something about it. These days, being stressed has become so normalized that we often neglect to do something about it. Especially in the workplace, being stressed has become the norm. So, we hide our stress, scared that if we admit that we're stressed, we'll appear weak. We feel like we *should* be able to cope with it, even though an impossible task is ahead of us (Ieso, 2020).

The truth is that stress shouldn't be as normalized as it is. Instead of viewing stress as *everyone's problem,* we must self-reflect and ask ourselves, *Why do I have it?* That's why we need to understand the signs and symptoms of stress. I spoke to a man in his thirties a while back who, mid-conversation, started experiencing an intense headache. I was about to take him to the emergency room when he said, "No, I'm fine. I've had them all my life. It's normal." I believed his first two statements: He has had it all of his life, and he is fine. But he lost me at the third statement. Normal? It may have become normalized in his daily life, but it's definitely not normal to have severe headaches daily. After a brief discussion, it was clear that his headaches were due to stress and that he'd become so used to it that he barely recognized that he was feeling stressed.

In this chapter, we'll take a closer look at the signs and symptoms of stress, as well as how self-awareness and acceptance can be used as tools to battle stress.

SIGNS AND SYMPTOMS OF STRESS

Similarly to burnout, stress affects us in different ways. It can affect our emotions, bodies, and behavior. Sometimes we might just feel a little *off* and not realize that it's because we are severely stressed. Let's have a look at the signs and symptoms of stress (Mind, 2017).

How Stress Can Make You Feel

- irritable
- angry
- impatient
- anxious
- afraid
- racing thoughts
- depressed
- unable to relax
- uninterested
- worried
- dreadful
- like you've lost your sense of humor
- lonely
- neglected

Physical Signs

- shallow breathing
- panic attacks
- blurred eyesight
- itchy eyes
- sleeping problems
- fatigue
- headaches
- muscle aches
- chest pain
- high blood pressure
- indigestion
- constipation or diarrhea
- dizziness
- weight fluctuation
- itchy skin
- sweating
- changes to the menstrual cycle

How Stress Can Make You Behave

- indecisiveness
- unable to concentrate
- unable to remember things
- feeling worried
- snapping at those around you

- nail-biting
- pick at your skin
- teeth grinding
- low libido
- change in eating habits
- feeling tearful
- overspending
- smoking and drinking

SELF-AWARENESS AS A TOOL AGAINST STRESS

Recognizing the above symptoms and acknowledging that you are being affected by stress, requires self-awareness. Having self-awareness means that you have a clear understanding of who you are, how you normally act and react, and what your strengths and weaknesses are (Whittleton, 2018). Self-awareness is the first step in fighting stress since it allows you to take control of your emotions, behaviors, and personality. The more self-awareness you have, the more likely you are to identify stress and engage in self-care behaviors to deal with the stress. According to Mark Manson, a well-known self-help author, self-awareness is the ability to "observe and accurately identify our thoughts, feelings, and impulses and determine whether they are grounded in reality or not" (2018). Let's take a quick look at some of the benefits of self-awareness (Manson, 2018).

Benefits of Self-Awareness

- Aids in self-control and self-esteem.
- Boosts creativity and pride.
- Helps with acceptance and proactivity.
- Facilitates decision-making.
- Leads to accurate self-reports.

Stress works in cycles of thought patterns. You think something that causes stress, which leads to more stressful thinking, and so the cycle continues. The best way to stop the cycle is by removing one of the dominos, causing a break in the cycle, and bringing it to a halt. Through self-awareness, you can stop the cycle of stressful thoughts. You become aware of your stressful thinking and stop the process before it can continue to spiral.

Signs That You Lack Self-Awareness

Before we look at some signs that might indicate you're lacking self-awareness, remember that we are all humans, and no one is perfect. If you have some of these signs, and you're able to point them out, give yourself a pat on the back because that means you are already one step closer to achieving self-awareness!

- You are always defensive.
- You are in denial about things in your personal and work life.
- You feel the need to micromanage people and situations.
- You make excuses and blame others when things go wrong.

If you're starting to realize that you might lack self-awareness, that's a good thing. If it's making you feel stressed or anxious, take a deep breath and know that self-awareness can be taught. You might lack self-awareness now, but that doesn't mean that you'll lack self-awareness forever. With the right exercises and techniques, you'll be able to learn self-awareness like a pro. Before we look at how to improve self-awareness, we need to discuss the different levels of self-awareness as described by Mark Manson (2018).

THREE LEVELS OF SELF-AWARENESS

Self-awareness is not just one thing that magically happens. There are levels to self-awareness, and in order to be fully self-aware, you need to understand the three levels.

The three levels are (Mason, 2018):

- Understanding what you're doing.
- Understanding what you're feeling.
- Knowing your blind spots.

Let's take a closer look at each of these three levels in order to identify how we can improve our self-awareness.

Level 1: What Am I Doing?

Take a moment and think back over the last 30 days and answer the following questions.

- How many times did I struggle with a relationship?
- How often did I feel lonely and isolated?
- Did I feel unproductive?
- How many times have I been underfed, tired, and low on energy?
- How often did I stress about work or finances?
- Was I uncertain about my future at all?
- How many times have I been physically ill or hurt?

If you count all of those times together, chances are that you'll have a near-perfect score. Do you know what that means? It means that for the past 30 days, every day has basically sucked. Usually, we avoid information like this by distracting ourselves through technology, entertainment, and anything that gives us a moment of delight. We all need some sort of diversion to keep us sane, but this often leads to a lack of self-awareness. That's why we need to check in with ourselves. We spend hours upon hours keeping ourselves busy with things that aren't fulfilling us; they're merely distracting us. Eventually, our distractions become compulsions. We're unable to go to bed without scrolling or be out in public without putting music on. These compulsions make us less aware of what we're actually doing with our lives and how we spend our time. The first level of self-awareness is becoming aware of what you're doing with your time.

Level 2: What Am I Feeling?

The second level of self-awareness is understanding what you're feeling. Usually, as soon as you become aware of how you spend your time and you start to remove distractions, you're faced with what you're feeling. All the feelings of rage, anger, and disappointment that you've been hiding for so long are suddenly overwhelming, leading you to smash your laptop mouse into tiny pieces or honk at the dude driving under the speed limit. That's why most of us keep ourselves distracted. We're terrified of being left alone with our feelings, but that's what the second level of self-awareness is about: Discovering how you really feel about yourself, your life, those around you, the weather, and everything in between. It's uncomfortable to be in level 2 because there's no hiding, and you might discover that you have feelings towards something that you don't want to, but it's in level 2 where you discover yourself more deeply.

The tricky thing is that oftentimes our emotions are just distractions from other distractions. I used to experience this all the time! Whenever I had to travel for work, I used to get annoyed with my family the night before. Like clockwork, I would start a fight with whoever annoyed me. When I became aware of this, I started investigating and realized that I was actually feeling sad. I didn't want to leave my family behind, but in order to distract myself from the sadness, I used annoyance and anger to cope with it. In order to be aware of your emotions, you must also know when to stop analyzing them; otherwise, you'll get stuck in a big loop of self-obsession (Mason, 2018).

Level 3: Where Are My Blindspots?

The third level of self-awareness is knowing where your blind spots are. We all have blind spots, and if you think you don't, that's probably yours. The more you are aware of yourself, the more you'll start to realize that you don't know everything. Let's say, for example, that you had a very bad day at work and fought with your colleagues. Later, you're watching a movie, but you're still thinking of the fight, so nothing is funny. So, you deem the movie trash. Level 3 of awareness is being able to spot these assumptions that you make. Instead of telling everyone what a crappy movie it is, tell them that you didn't enjoy it because you had a crappy day. You don't have to be perfect all the time, as long as you are aware of the fact that your judgment was clouded.

IMPROVING YOUR SELF-AWARENESS

If the first step of self-awareness is knowing that you need self-awareness, we're halfway there! However, there's more to it than just knowing you need better self-awareness. It's like knowing you're hungry and actually picking up the phone to order food. Self-awareness can be improved through different activities, and next, we'll discuss five ways in which you can cultivate more self-awareness (Ackerman, 2021).

What Are You Doing?	How?
Create space and time	• Take five minutes every day to connect with yourself. • Avoid digital distractions. • Allow yourself time to be completely alone and in solitude.
Practice mindfulness	• Take note of your feelings as they arise. • Be present when walking, eating, talking, and listening.
Journal your awareness	• Use a journal to process your thoughts through writing. • Write down how you are feeling and why.
Practice listening	• When someone is talking, focus on listening without distractions. • Observe your emotions and body language as you interact with others.
Gain a different perspective	• Ask for feedback and ask someone you trust to point out your blind spots.

ACCEPTING UNCERTAINTY AND ADVERSITY

Besides self-awareness, another great tool to battle stress is learning how to accept uncertainty and adversity. Life is filled with events and experiences that we don't plan for. Whether it's a global pandemic or sudden financial pressure, we're surrounded by uncertainty and adversity on a daily basis. As humans, we crave security, and when we fail to feel secure, we start to panic and slip into a downward spiral of *what-ifs* (Robinson & Smith, 2020). We all deal with adversity in our own way, and we have different tolerance levels for uncertainty. However, we all have a limit. At some point, uncertainty and adversity become overwhelming, and we start to worry. That's why it's so important for all of us to learn how to deal with uncertainty.

As much as we may want to maneuver away from it, uncertainty is unavoidable and part of our lives. Nothing we do can remove uncertainty 100%. Even if you pack your bags and move to a remote island where you stay in a small hut all by yourself in the mountains, you will be faced with uncertainty. A bear might show up at your front door, or perhaps the weather would surprise you with an unexpected rainstorm. The point is no one can hide from uncertainty, so why don't we just learn how to deal with it? We spend so much time worrying about things we can't control and preparing for *what-ifs*. What if we instead took that energy and invested it in learning new techniques for accepting uncertainty and adversity? Well, that's exactly what we're going to do right now. There are five steps to overcoming uncertainty and adversity (Cameron, 2022).

Stop Arguing With Reality

Have you ever been in an argument, and mid-way through, you realize that it's impossible to win? Isn't that the most frustrating thing ever? Well, that's exactly what we do when we argue with reality. No matter what the circumstances, if you argue with reality, you're going to lose. You need to see things as they are if you want to live a life that's not ruled by fear and anxiety. Take a look at what you're going through in life currently and analyze it based on facts and the truth. Don't obsess about the *what-if's* and the *could have's* and *should have's*. Reality can be your best friend during stressful times. Do you know why? Because reality helps you focus on the things that you can control. By focusing on reality, you take back your power.

Stop Thinking the Worst

It's fun thinking up worst-case scenarios. Well, fun as in it's easy and in a weird way, it makes us feel better temporarily, but not fun as in I'm enjoying my time here on earth. The thing is, your mind is a bit of a drama queen. Have a headache? It must be a tumor! An impromptu meeting with the boss? Getting fired, for sure. Haven't you heard back from your best friend? It's because she actually hates you. These are all examples of ways that our minds overreact and act a little dramatic. To get yourself out of a fatalistic mindset, take a moment and ask yourself, *So what*? What is the worst thing that can possibly happen? Then ask yourself whether this is really as bad as it looks. When you focus on the problems, it will constantly leave you feeling drained. However, if you focus on the solution, it will give you the energy to come up with better outcomes (Cameron, 2022).

Remember, misery loves company, and that's why some people never seem to get out of their problems. We become addicted to drama, and we subconsciously start thinking of ways to create more. Take a break. Take a deep breath and stop thinking the worst.

Don't Beat Yourself Up

Uncertainty is also proficient in the *It's all your fault* game. When you're uncertain about things, you can quickly slip into the trap of blame and guilt. The problem is that neither of these emotions is serving you positively in any way. So, how about instead of feeling guilty or shameful, you take back the power by taking responsibility? Take a moment, forgive yourself, and move on. Learn and grow from the experiences you're having, and stop the guilt before you fall into the trap of playing the victim. Believe me; you are smarter and stronger than you think. Instead of beating yourself up, ask yourself how you can grow from this experience and uncertainty (Cameron, 2022).

Stop the Lies

Uncertainty is like a computer that refuses to update its software. Whenever we're faced with uncertainty, we tend to fall back into old habits and thinking patterns. No matter how much therapy you get or how often you read self-help books, your original programming is always waiting for an opportunity to shine. In order to upgrade the system, you need to identify the lies that you are telling yourself and stop repeating them. If you're used to believing that you're not good enough, as soon as you hit a bump in the road, your brain will automatically jump to the conclusion that this uncertainty happened because you're not good enough. You have to pay close attention to these thought patterns and actively fight it by doing a manual override. When the lie is that you think you're not good enough, look for evidence that this is not true. Where have you achieved success in your life? Focus on reality instead of feeding the lie (Cameron, 2022).

Be Honest

When you're honest with yourself, you will discover the truth. The truth will lead you to let go of uncertainty and adversity and accept it for what it is: uncontrollable and unpredictable. According to experts, it takes nine positive statements to override every negative statement (Cameron, 2022). This means that for every uncertainty that you worry about, you need to think at least nine positive thoughts. If you're currently overwhelmed with uncertainty, it might be because your ratio is off. Take some time and think about all the uncertainty that you're currently stressed about and replace it with truths.

By letting go of uncertainty and becoming more self-aware, we can manage our stress and anxiety better. Instead of feeling overwhelmed, we can use these tools to take back our thoughts and regain control over the things that we can control. In the next chapter, we'll chat more about the different stress triggers and how you can recognize when you are being triggered by stress. Before we look into that, it's time to take the stress away.

WRITING THE STRESS AWAY

For this chapter's journaling moment, I want you to use the following two methods to identify your current stressful thoughts. I recommend writing these techniques down in your journal for future reference. Over the next couple of days, whenever you are feeling stressed, refer to these techniques and give them a try. These two techniques were adapted from Carol Vivyan, a Cognitive Behavioral Psychotherapist and author (2019).

ABCDE Technique

	Explanation	Check ✓
A: **A**ttention	As soon as you feel stressed about something, stop and ask yourself what you are paying attention to right now. What is your mind telling you?	
B: **B**elieve	Don't just believe your thoughts because they are yours. Not all thoughts are correct.	
C: **C**hallenge	Defuse your stress by challenging your thoughts. Is there a bigger picture? What might make you feel calmer?	
D: **D**iscount	Recognize that your stress is overwhelming you, and let the unhelpful thoughts go. By doing this, you are removing the power that stress has over you.	
E: **E**xplore Options	What would be helpful to focus on right now? Is there something else that might be better to think about?	

Think Technique

	Explanation	Check ✓
T: **T**rue	Is this thought true? What are the facts?	
H: **H**elpful	Is paying attention to this thought helpful in any way?	
I: **I**nspiring	Does this thought inspire you, or does it have the opposite effect?	
N: **N**ecessary	Is it necessary to act on this thought right now?	
K: **K**ind	Is the thought kind?	

4

RECOGNIZE YOUR TRIGGERS

Have you ever experienced feeling absolutely relaxed one minute and sick with anxiety the next? This is something that I've experienced so often in my life. One moment I would be there and present, and the next, I'd be unable to hold a conversation without bringing up work. One of the worst cases I had was during a holiday trip with my family. We were all having a blast, relaxing next to the pool while taking a quick swim whenever the sun got too warm. One moment I was laughing, and the next moment I saw a man sitting with his laptop near the pool. I don't even know what the man was doing, but I immediately assumed that he was working, which triggered guilt in me. I suddenly started thinking of all the work that I still needed to do and how busy I was going to be when I got home. I started panicking and was convinced that I had forgotten to set an *out-of-office* email response before I left. I was so anxious that I got out of the pool, walked to our hotel room, and started working for a couple of hours. Did it make me feel better? For a couple of moments, sure. Was it better than spending quality time with my family? Definitely not. So, what happened? That, my friend, is the perfect example of being triggered.

Triggers also referred to as "stressors," can be anything that causes your brain to release stress hormones (Centre for Studies on Human Stress, 2019). Triggers can be broadly categorized into four groups: physiological, Psychological, Psychosocial, and Psychospiritual. In this chapter, we'll take a look at the different types of triggers, why it's important to recognize your triggers, and how you respond to these triggers. Let's start by taking a closer look at the four different types of triggers.

TYPES OF TRIGGERS

Stress has been linked as a cofactor in 95% of all diseases (Friedman, 2015). Do you know what that means? It means that 95% of people who struggle with some sort of disease can partly blame stress for it. Not only is that statistic enough to make everyone realize the importance of dealing with stress, but it should also motivate you to find a way of releasing the pent-up stress that you carry with you. The process of preventing stress from ruling your life starts with identifying the stress factors as one of four types.

Physiological

Physiological stress, also known as physical stress, is a type of stressor that puts strain on your physical body. Physiological triggers are things that happen to you physically that can cause stress in your life.

Physiological triggers include

- trauma like surgery or injury
- intense physical labor
- environmental pollution
- illness
- low blood sugar
- inadequate light
- noise
- radiation
- fatigue
- biochemical imbalance
- dietary stress
- dehydration
- allergies
- substance abuse

- dental challenges
- musculoskeletal misalignment

Psychological

While physiological stress influences our physical bodies, psychological stress is often caused by events and situations that we interpret as negative. This happens mentally and doesn't necessarily have a physical impact.

Psychological triggers include

- emotional stress
- cognitive stress
- anxiety
- panic attacks
- shame
- jealousy
- grief
- perceptual stress
- rumors
- self-loathing
- information overload

Psychosocial

Psychosocial stress impacts the social aspects of your life. It causes stress in the areas where you interact with others or, in some cases, lack interaction with others.

Psychosocial triggers include

- relationship difficulties
- marriage difficulties
- problems with children
- lack of social support
- lack of resources for adequate survival
- loss of a loved one
- bankruptcy
- isolation

Psychospiritual

While psychosocial stress influences your interpersonal relationships, psychospiritual stress is caused by a lack of spiritual meaning or purpose. Even if you are not a religious person, spirituality is an important aspect of mental health. When you have psychospiritual triggers, you might experience additional stress without understanding why. Psychospiritual triggers include

- A crisis of values
- Feeling as if life has no meaning
- Lack of purpose
- Joyless striving
- Misalignment with core beliefs

No matter the type of stress, prolonged stress can result in serious issues, so it's important to catch triggers before they spiral into a whole world of anxiety-driven behavior and thoughts. In the previous chapter, we spoke about how self-awareness can help with stress reduction, but another tool that is useful when dealing with stress is to identify the thoughts that trigger you to stress and find a healthy way of dealing with them. Let's take a look at some thoughts that might trigger stress in your life.

THOUGHTS THAT MIGHT TRIGGER STRESS

Although we are all different and deal with stress differently, there are a couple of stressors that most of us experience, like stress regarding other people, money, work, our physical bodies, our minds, leisure, and life trauma. However, sometimes it's not the event itself that causes us stress, but the thoughts that come with it (Lukowski, 2019). For example, it's not the mistake in your work that causes stress, but the thought that now your boss will be angry and probably fire you. What you think during certain situations is incredibly important and more powerful than what you realize. In the table below, you'll find a scenario with a hypothetical event and, next to it, the thoughts that might come with it that are actually the source of stress. The beauty of this is that even though you cannot control the event, you can control your thoughts, which means that it's a stress that you can get rid of with the right amount of self-awareness.

The Scenario	The Thoughts
Your long-time partner calls things off.	You assume that it's because you're a terrible person and that they never really loved you instead of seeing that you've grown apart.
You make a mistake at work.	You believe that you are the worst employee ever, completely incompetent, and your boss will fire you as soon as he finds out.
You struggle with depressive and intrusive thoughts.	You assume that you can't change the way you think, and you'll always struggle with this.
Someone makes a comment about you looking tired and asks whether you've been crying.	You think that crying and being tired are weaknesses because others will point them out and embarrass you.
Someone criticizes your outfit.	You assume that you've done something wrong.
You feel overwhelmed and contemplate asking for help.	You change your mind because strong people don't ask for help.
You get a bad deal, and someone takes advantage of your situation.	You're mad because the world is supposed to be fair.
Your life is spinning out of control, and you have to run around to get everything done.	You think that everything is under your control.
You have a disagreement with a friend.	You think that they must see the world the same way you do; otherwise, you won't be able to solve the issues.

As you can see, the scenario usually gets blamed for the fact that we experience stress, but in reality, it is our thinking that is to blame. The way you respond to a stressful situation and the thoughts that you have can determine whether you are adding to your stress or managing it in a way that is healthy. One of the best skills you can learn is how to stop blaming the situation you're in and instead focus on your reactions. For many years, I blamed my situation for everything. I used to think that the hypothetical scenarios above were to blame for my stress and failures when in reality, it was my own thinking that was the problem. After many years of believing that my thoughts were not the problem, I finally saw the light and started working on being aware of stressors and my reactions, not just the things that I thought would cause me stress.

BEING AWARE OF YOUR STRESSORS AND REACTIONS

To reduce the negative effects of stress on your life, you need to recognize your stressors (triggers) and be aware of your reactions to these stressors (Lawson, 2016). Research has developed four steps for becoming aware of your stressors as well as your reactions. Similar to self-awareness practices from the previous chapter, this is a type of self-awareness exercise that will help you to take it a level further than before and identify your reaction towards stress.

Step 1: What Are Your Sources?

The first step is to find the source of your stress. Identify whether it's a physiological, psychological, psychosocial, or psychospiritual stressor. Take some time and check in with yourself. Ask yourself how you are feeling and pay close attention to the abovementioned four areas. How do you feel physically, mentally, spiritually, and socially? Can you identify problems that might be causing stress in any of those four areas? Acknowledge your feelings without guilt or trying to think of a solution. Just allow yourself to feel and become aware.

Step 2: What Can You Do About It?

As soon as you're aware of what you're feeling and where the stress is located, you can start thinking about what you can do about it. Start by asking yourself the following questions:

- Can I avoid this stress?
- Do I have any conflict that I need to resolve?
- Can I prepare for any stressful situations in advance?
- Can I practice self-compassion and not be too hard on myself?
- Do I have any unhelpful thoughts that are contributing to the stress?

By answering these questions, you'll start to become aware of your thoughts regarding the problem and whether the stress might actually be in your thinking and not the issue itself. If you can eliminate stress by becoming aware of it, then you can also use awareness to take action and recognize which of your thought patterns need changing (Lawson, 2016).

Step 3: How Do You Experience Stress?

Up next, it's time to ask yourself how you usually react when you are stressed. Answering these questions truthfully is essential since this is not about giving the perfect answer but about identifying whether your reaction is contributing to your stress. Let me give you this example.

I worked with a young man a couple of years ago who had an extremely short temper. He was a wonderful guy, usually extremely kind and helpful, but if he felt cornered or teamed up against, he would lose his cool. Afterward, he would feel terrible and be mad at himself for reacting in such a way. He once got into an argument with one of his colleagues, and instead of walking away, he started yelling back. The two had a full-on screaming match in the middle of the office, and both got written warnings. As I spoke to him about it, he said, "If only I had kept my cool, it would have been over by now." His reaction (the screaming back) to the original stress (conflict with a colleague) ended up being more stressful than the original situation. After a couple of sessions, he was able to identify how his reactions made the stress worse and has been working on his anger ever since.

Do you see now why it's important to be mindful of how you react in certain situations? Start by asking yourself the following questions:

- How do you react when you feel stressed?
- Do you become irritable when feeling stressed?
- How does your body feel when you're stressed?
- What negative thoughts do you seem to jump to when stressed?

Step 4: How Do You Cope?

The final step is identifying how you cope with stress on a regular basis. Do you attempt to eat away your stress? Or perhaps you're like me when I was on holiday, trying to work away the stress? It's important that you truly identify your coping mechanisms, both the unhealthy and healthy ones. After you've identified your coping mechanisms, ask yourself: Do I feel better afterward or more stressed? I can honestly tell you that working away from stress only helps temporarily, but spending time with family has a long-term effect.

RESPONDING TO STRESS

Most people respond to stress differently. While my brother used to gym away his stress, I would use books and fantasy worlds to get away from stress. If you're not sure how you respond to stress, here's a list of common ways that people react to stress, adapted from the CMHS (Office of Mental Health, 2000). Go through the list and check no more than ten common reactions that you have to stress.

✓	**Reaction to Stress**
	Change in activity levels
	Decreased effectiveness
	Difficulty communicating
	Irritability and outbursts
	Dark sense of humor
	Change in eating habits
	Periods of crying
	Increased use of drugs and alcohol
	Change in sleep
	Denial
	Anxiety and panic
	Vivid dreams
	Guilt and shame
	Feeling overwhelmed
	Feeling misunderstood

	Apathy
	Increased heart rate
	Upset stomach
	Muffled hearing
	Tremors
	Sweating or chills
	Headaches
	Lower back pain
	Change in sexual desires
	Hair loss
	Isolation
	Difficulty sharing ideas
	Criticizing
	Loss of objectivity
	Limited attention span
	Confusion
	Easily startled
	Forgetfulness
	Allergies
	Change in the menstrual cycle
	Aching muscles
	Tunnel vision
	Worry about safety for self and others

The Three Stages

According to Marathon Health (2020), your perception of stress matters more than the stressor itself. Most of us experience General Adaptation Syndrome when confronted with stress. General Adaptation Syndrome is your body's response to stress, and it consists of three stages.

1. **The alarm stage**: The first step is when the nervous system is awakened and tells your body to prepare for something bad.
2. **The resistance stage**: Your body begins to repair itself after the initial shock of the stressful event and enters the recovery stage.
3. **The exhaustion stage**: This happens when the first two stages continue, causing an unbalance in your body. This is where diseases begin.

Five Responses

As I mentioned earlier, we all respond to stress differently. This isn't just something I say to sound inclusive and welcoming; it's actually also scientific. According to research, there are five responses to stress that our bodies use to protect us from harm, commonly referred to as the "five-F's of stress" (RCEW, n.d.). Let's take a look at the five in the context of seeing a wild dog that looks like it might want to bite you.

THE FIVE-F'S: THE RESPONSE

The Five-F's	The Response
Fight	When you go into *fight mode*, you prepare to stand your ground and fight your way out of the situation. You're ready to kick the dog in the throat if need be.
Flight	You immediately put distance between you and the dog by running away and finding a tree to climb.
Freeze	You freeze, and your entire body goes still. It's almost considered *playing dead* to avoid further potential harm. You quietly sit still, hoping the dog will lose interest.
Flop	Your muscles go floppy and jelly, and you're unable to control your thoughts. This is your body's way of shutting down to reduce pain.
Friend	You call for help. As you see the dog run up to you, you start screaming, or you plead with the dog to stop.

Now that you understand the importance of identifying your response to stress and know the different ways in which people might respond, you can start to identify how you react to stress and how your thoughts might contribute to feeling anxious and stressed. In the next chapter, we'll talk more about cutting down on overthinking and how overthinking contributes to stress. First, it's time for another journaling moment and practical exercise.

WRITE THE STRESS AWAY

Identify an event in your life that was stressful:	**How did you respond to the stress?**
Did your thoughts make the stress worse or better?	**How can you improve your response in the future?**

5

CUT DOWN ON OVERTHINKING

I would like to introduce you to my best friend, Rob. Rob and I grew up together, and we've been friends since middle school. When you look at Rob now, you'll see a successful businessman who created his own adventure business where he takes tourists on various adrenaline-rush activities. You see a man who is confident, kind, and self-assured. It's funny because if you knew Rob in middle school, you wouldn't recognize him! I often tease him about it because he has transformed so much since then. Sure, he started working out more and started paying more attention to his style, but the area in which he transformed the most was his anxiety.

You see, Rob was an extreme overthinker, and I don't mean overthinker as in he couldn't decide what to order in the restaurant; overthinking as in getting paralyzed by fear before jumping in the pool because what if his legs started cramping and he drowns. In fact, on Rob's fourteenth birthday, he refused to eat his birthday cake because it had peanut butter in the buttercream, and he was terrified that he had developed a peanut allergy overnight. When you look at the bungee-jumping, skydiving Rob now, it's hard to remember such an anxious boy. But just like his peanut butter allergy didn't develop overnight, neither did his confidence. It took a lot of effort, intentionality, and input to get rid of his overthinking, but he did it, and you can too.

In this chapter, we'll talk all about overthinking and how it contributes to stress. We'll discuss what it is, the signs of overthinking, as well as the causes. Lastly, we'll look at ways to stop overthinking and find peace of mind yet again.

WHAT IS OVERTHINKING?

Overthinking is like being stuck on a hamster wheel. You run and run and run, yet you get nowhere. With overthinking, you think about the same thought over and over again, analyzing the simplest of situations until all sense of proportion is gone (Daltrey, 2016). Whenever you overthink a problem, it gets bigger and bigger, and your brain simply cannot find a positive outcome for the magnitude of the problem, which results in anxiety and severe stress. Over the last couple of years, the term *overthinking* has been floating around social media quite lightheartedly. People say things like, "overthinking my text response" or "overthinking my holiday packing." It's funny and all until you actually struggle with overthinking, and no one seems to get that it's serious.

Overthinking can also be referred to as *rumination.* When you are unable to let go of something that happened years ago, and you replay that memory over and over, thinking of everything that you could've done differently, you are most likely an overthinker. I remember when Rob and I were little. One moment we'd be climbing trees, and the next, he would freak out about something he told a teacher three years ago or remember how he embarrassed himself at the school dance months ago. This is the perfect example of overthinking—getting stuck in those past memories or perhaps even getting stuck in the uncertainty of the future. When something extreme happens, the average person would feel embarrassed, plan to apologize and make it right, and then move on by dinner time the next evening. For overthinkers, that embarrassment will continue to haunt you for years to come if you don't deal with it.

Overthinking comes from the primitive emotional part of the brain, which tends to see things from the worst possible perspective. The brain is hyper-vigilant and is trying to keep you alive; it sees the embarrassment as life-threatening. In some ways, overthinking is replaying worst-case scenarios, being unable to move on, and being completely stuck in the sense of helplessness and stress.

SIGNS OF OVERTHINKING

Overthinking can be hard to spot since it often disguises itself as self-reflection and problem-solving. You can easily convince yourself that you're thinking about the past in order to get a better response for the future or because you're self-reflecting on your behavior. The difference is that with both problem-solving and self-reflection, you are looking for specific answers; you're not just replaying the memory to point out everything you did wrong or to get stuck in negativity.

Although overthinking can be hard to spot, there are definite signs, which include:

- Dwelling on the past.
- Second-guessing every decision you've ever made.

- Replay all the mistakes you've ever made.
- Rehashing challenging conversations.
- Fixating on things you can't control.
- Imagining the worst-case scenarios.
- Questioning yourself but never taking action.
- Constantly replaying *what-if* questions.
- Inability to focus on anything other than what worries you.

CAUSES OF OVERTHINKING

Overthinking is not considered a mental illness in itself, although it is associated with conditions such as depression, anxiety, eating disorders, and substance abuse. For some people, overthinking happens as a response to chronic pain or illness. When you're faced with pain on a daily basis, it can be very difficult to think about anything other than the pain, leading to overthinking. The negative thoughts that constantly occupy the mind as a result of pain can be extremely overwhelming. According to Natalie Dattilo, a clinical health psychologist, many people have the impression that worrying about something shows that you care, which is why it can easily become an unhealthy habit (Acosta, 2022). It's essential that you identify the cause of your overthinking in order to prevent it from continuing. Working as a psychologist, Nick Wignall identified seven reasons why people tend to overthink (2021). Let's take a closer look at each of the causes.

Childhood Learning

Interestingly enough, most people who struggle with overthinking developed the habit as children. Take my friend, Rob, for example. He started struggling with overthinking from an extremely young age. According to Wignall (2021), most children develop overthinking as a way to deal with scary and difficult experiences. If a child has to deal with an alcoholic parent or a parent that fights often, they might start to obsessively worry about what would happen if the parents started fighting again or if dad came home drunk. Thinking of these scenarios obsessively might quite literally keep them out of harm's way. The thing is, once the habit is developed, it continues long after the threat has been dealt with. It's also important to know that the initial cause of your overthinking can be very different from the reason for maintaining the habit (Wignall, 2021).

Chasing Control

Most humans hate feeling helpless. This is especially true when people close to us experience suffering. We want to help them, but we don't have control over the situation. Instead of accepting that the situation is out of our control, we live in denial and constantly think about the problem. It's not helpful at all, but at least we feel like we're being helpful because it occupies our minds. Despite the slight relief we feel when we constantly worry about others, the long-term cost isn't worth it and can lead to severe chronic anxiety. If you want to stop overthinking, you have to accept that you cannot control everything.

Craving Certainty

The illusion of clarity is the illusion of control's sibling. As human beings, we love knowing what is going to happen next. We crave clarity, and our confidence depends on how certain we are of something. Oftentimes, we feel so anxious about not having certainty that we keep ourselves stuck in problem-solving mode. We lie to ourselves about the state of clarity by thinking that if we think about the problem long enough, we'll gain new insight. Of course, that is very rarely the case, and living with uncertainty is part of the human experience (Wignall, 2021).

Perfectionism

Perfectionism has nothing to do with being perfect and everything to do with feeling perfect. If you struggle with perfectionism, you have a hard time moving on because you don't feel perfect about it yet. Perfectionism ends up as overthinking because it is an obsession to feel perfect in everything that you do (Wignall, 2021). If you struggle with overthinking, it might be because you are a perfectionist, and the only way you can deal with perfectionism is by accepting that sometimes you might feel inadequate, and that's okay.

Secondary Gain

A lot of people get stuck in overthinking because it has a secondary gain. A secondary gain is when you get a non-obvious benefit from the experience. For example, you might continue to overthink because it leads to sympathy and pity from others. If you continuously overthink, you're probably getting something out of it (Wignall, 2021). I encourage you to sit down and ask yourself what you gain from overthinking because, a lot of the time, secondary gain happens subconsciously. The best way to change the habit of overthinking is to understand your reasoning for overthinking in the first place.

Overgeneralization

Some people struggle with overthinking since they assume that if a lot of thinking helps in one area of life, it must surely work in the rest as well. For example, if you're a student, you will understand that a lot of thinking is very beneficial during exams, so generalize that a lot of thinking is always helpful, which leads to overthinking. Since thinking is considered a tool, it can sometimes be hard to find the balance between when to use the tool and when to put it down. To an expert thinker, everything looks like a problem that can be solved through thinking (Wignall, 2021). Ask yourself whether more analytical thinking is really required before spiraling down the overthinking rabbit hole.

Fear of Conflict

While avoiding conflict is normal for most people, some people take it to the extreme. The problem is that the more you avoid conflict, the less you practice dealing with conflict, which makes you avoid conflict even more. Not all conflict is bad, and dealing with conflict in a healthy manner is actually very beneficial. However, the fear of conflict might send you into a state of overthinking where you determine that all conflict is bad, so you continue to avoid it. When you avoid external conflict, you often struggle more with internal conflict (Wignall, 2021). Avoiding conflict can often be more stressful than just facing it and having a normal conversation about it.

I remember when Rob and I were teenagers, there was a week when I didn't talk to Rob much. I thought we were just busy with school stuff, and I didn't even realize that he was actually avoiding me. After a week, he came up to me, furious that I hadn't even realized that he was mad. Ironically, he spent the entire week being mad at me but avoiding conflict because he was scared of it. As soon as he spoke to me about it, we resolved the issue within five minutes. What could've taken only five minutes of his time turned into an entire week of internal conflict and frustration.

HOW TO STOP OVERTHINKING

Even if you've struggled with overthinking since you were a child, you can overcome it. Overthinking is just a habit, and although habits can be strong, they are breakable. With the right plan of action, you can stop overthinking and let go of anxiety. Let's take a look at five ways to stop overthinking (Lamothe, 2022).

Take a Step Back

The first way that you can avoid overthinking is by taking a step back and analyzing how you respond to stress, which you can tick off your list since we did that in the previous chapter. Taking a step back when you start to overthink can be tricky, but it's not impossible. I asked Rob his opinion on dealing with overthinking, and he agreed that stepping back is a great first step. He continued by explaining that he usually practices the lead character method. He removes himself from the situation and then imagines his current life and situation as if he is watching a movie. It's easy to give good advice to movie characters when you don't have to actually follow the advice. So, pretend like you're watching a movie, get objectivity, and then listen to the advice that you give your main character-self.

Find a Healthy Distraction

In some cases, the best way to deal with overthinking is by finding a healthy distraction. The key word here is *healthy*. Finding a healthy distraction and procrastination is not the same thing. Healthy distractions include activities like learning to cook, going to a workout class, or volunteering at a local charity. With a simple 30-minute distraction, you can stop overthinking thoughts and focus your energy on something that serves you and does not harm you (Wignall, 2021). Whenever I start to feel a wave of overthinking coming on, I go swimming. Being physically active gives my brain something else to focus on and also helps my body relax.

Breathing Exercise

Meditation is another way to prevent overthinking from continuing. If you're thinking of meditation as sitting cross-legged in your garden next to a stack of rocks and going, *uhmm...*, you're missing the point slightly. Sure, some meditation techniques include these practices, but some meditation techniques are as simple as breathing deeply. If you've never meditated in your life, breathing exercises are a great way to start! Breathing clears your mind, and it physically calms your body (Wignall, 2021). By breathing deeply, you disengage from fight-or-flight mode, which means that your mind gets to relax and think more objectively. Here's a beginner-friendly breathing exercise that you can start with.

Beginner-Friendly Breathing Exercise	
Step 1	Find a comfortable place to sit. Relax your neck and shoulders.
Step 2	Place one hand on your belly and the other on your heart.
Step 3	Inhale and exhale through your nose. Pay attention to how your chest and stomach are moving.
Step 4	Repeat for five minutes. Journal how you are feeling afterwards.

Look at the Bigger Picture

Looking at the bigger picture is another way that you can stop your overthinking mind from taking complete control. Simply close your eyes, focus on the problem at hand, and ask yourself: *How will this affect me in five years? Will this matter in a couple of months? Does this influence my future?* Chances are, a lot of the time, the answer will be no. This technique helps you let go of minor issues and not turn them into large obstacles (Wignall, 2021).

ANTs

Automatic negative thoughts (ANTs) are knee-jerk negative thoughts that usually involve feelings of fear and anger (Wignall, 2021). It's your initial reaction to a situation that usually sends you into overthinking mode. By tackling your ANTs, you take back the power and change your knee-jerk reaction from one of negativity to one of positivity. You can work through your ANTs by keeping a record of your emotions and identifying ways that you can change them. Use the following steps to tackle your ANTs.

Dealing With Automatic Negative Thoughts	
Step 1	Write down in your journal what is making you anxious or affecting your mood. Write down the first thing that comes to your mind.
Step 2	Dig into the details and evaluate why this situation activated a negative response.
Step 3	Break down the different emotions that you are feeling by identifying what exactly you're experiencing.
Step 4	Find an alternative thought. Instead of jumping straight to "I'm a failure," replace it with "I'm trying my best."

There are hundreds of ideas online on how to deal with overthinking, but these five techniques are a great starting point. In the next chapter, we'll talk more about how time can influence stress and anxiety, but for now, let's do another writing exercise to finish off the chapter properly.

WRITE THE STRESS AWAY

This chapter's journaling time is all about identifying moments of overthinking and finding healthy ways to deal with them. Take some time to think about the questions below and use this template as a journaling prompt to help you discover the areas that you are overthinking.

What have I been overthinking lately?	
What steps can I take to stop overthinking?	
What are the things that I should let go of?	
Pros of overthinking:	**Cons of overthinking:**

6

KEEP AN EYE

Have you ever run out of time? Most of us run out of time on a daily basis! Between appointments, an insane workload, tests, family responsibilities, keeping the house clean, and taking a second to breathe, it's easy to lose track of time. Keeping an eye on the time is not just a cute little rhyme or a nice way to live. It can actually reduce your stress and help you manage your workload. Time management is an incredibly important tool to combat stress since it takes control of where you are and what you are doing. It can also help you improve your productivity, giving you more time to rest and recover. Poor time management is actually one of the biggest causes of stress (Shah, 2016). When you have poor time management, you might end up feeling anxious and stressed when, in reality, you don't really have much to do.

That's why this chapter is dedicated to time management, the advantages that time management has on our mental health, and practical ways in which we can get more managed in our lives. Part of time management is also organization. Being organized is not just a nice habit; it can actually make a big difference in our daily lives. Let's take a closer look at time management and organization.

INEFFECTIVE TIME MANAGEMENT

A lot of people think that poor time management means that you miss deadlines, but in truth, there is much more to time management. I know people who are terrible at time management and have never missed a deadline in their lives. However, they are constantly stressed, oversleep, run late for meetings, and look chaotic.

If you're not sure about your time management, here are a few signs that you might have poor time management (Shah, 2016):

- irritability
- mood swings

- tiredness
- inability to focus
- mental block
- memory lapses
- forgetfulness
- lack of sleep
- withdrawal
- depression

When you lack proper time management, your brain will find it difficult to switch off. You'll constantly think about work, scared that there won't be enough time to accomplish things. With proper time management techniques, you can organize projects and resting periods in such a way that you have enough time for everything, and you'll know when to do what. Poor time management practices can have effects that spill into every aspect of your life. In severe cases, it can lead to physical and mental problems (Levendusky, 2022). Let's take a look at a few ways that ineffective time management can influence our mental health.

Stress

Without time management, you don't know what to expect out of your day and week. You're not sure whether you'll have time for everything or when to do what. So, subconsciously, your brain is constantly in stress mode, preventing you from resting and recovering. This often leads to sudden waves of panic and guilt when resting or being unable to stop mid-project, scared that you won't have time to finish it. When you are constantly in stress mode, cortisol is released, and you'll constantly be in fight or flight mode.

Anxiety and Depression

Bad time management habits often lead to anxiety. When you have a lot of pending deadlines and unmet work quotas, the pressure can contribute to anxiety. The more the pressure piles up, the more anxious you'll get, leading you to feel imbalanced and unsatisfied with life. A big part of time management is allowing time for yourself. When you don't have time for yourself, you'll often feel lost and isolated (Levendusky, 2022). With ineffective time management, you fail to decompress and relax, leading to feelings of depression.

Poor Sleep Quality

The less you manage your time, the more you'll lack boundaries, especially if you work remotely. Working remotely is great because it offers you a lot of freedom, but it can also cause you to never leave your office and work ridiculous hours, neglecting your sleep quality. Poor sleep quality doesn't only leave you slightly sleepy it also influences the way you think about life and can drastically affect your mood. With good time management, you need to make sure that you schedule enough time to sleep in order to deliver your best work (Levendusky, 2022).

Burnout

Poor time management can contribute to burnout on many levels. When you're constantly battling personal- and work-life balance, you might start to experience burnout. Juggling too many things at once often leaves us feeling fatigued, which is acceptable every now and then, but if you're constantly tired, burnout might be starting to settle in. With proper time management, you can ensure that you have time for everything and everyone, setting up boundaries to prevent burnout.

So, how exactly does good time management contribute to mental health? Well, there are many benefits to effective time management (Andrews, 2022):

- You don't have to constantly worry about your progress because you have a clear plan and milestones, minimizing the effect of stress.
- You'll get enough sleep and rest by not putting off going to bed or changing your sleep schedule frequently.
- It can help you to avoid feeling overwhelmed, knowing what is expected and when you're

planning on doing what.
- You'll be more in control and less like a headless chicken running around in a desperate attempt to survive.
- It helps you to live a healthier life by prioritizing actions that contribute to your future and well-being.

MANAGE TIME TO REDUCE STRESS

Now that we understand just how bad poor time management can be, it's time to take a few practical steps toward improving our time management. I promise you that no matter how terrible your current time management situation is, it can be improved! Be warned, though; it won't magically happen overnight. In fact, it might even require a lot of hard work over several weeks, but it will be worth it. Thanks to the Palo Alto Medical Foundation (2019), we have five ways to improve our time management that have been medically proven to be successful.

Learn to Say "No"

The first step to better time management is learning how to say no. Saying no can be hard, especially if you have to say no to things or people you love. However, you need to say no to some things in order to say yes to the right things. If you say yes to everyone and everything, you'll soon be left with a full schedule and very little time to do the things you actually enjoy doing.

Realistic Schedules

The next step is to plan a schedule that is realistic. Don't schedule a coffee meeting with your best friend whom you haven't seen in two months, only 30 minutes. Not only will it not stay within those 30 minutes, but it will also steal the joy of catching up because you'll be stressed about other stuff. A realistic schedule includes time for exercise, relaxation, sleep, and laughter. Scheduling exercise and sleep are important because they are often the things that get pushed aside when our schedules are too full.

To-Do Lists

Begin each morning with a to-do list that is organized according to priority. Start by doing things that will only take a couple of minutes, and get those out of the way. Then, do the two things that are most important for the day. If you have time left, fill it with the things you have to do next. Whatever is left over, make sure those go on the priority list for tomorrow. Having a to-do list will help you to determine where you need to focus your attention and where your good stress should be focused on.

Combine Tasks and Errands

For the sake of efficiency, combine your tasks and errands. For example, if you have to go to a specific part of town for work-related things, call your friend who lives nearby and catch up over coffee. Combining errands with tasks can save you a lot of time, and it can help you to catch a few relaxation sessions in-between your busy schedule. Make sure to plan your errands a week in advance to make sure that you cover everything in one trip to maximize your time.

Plan Ahead

The final step in managing your time better is planning ahead. Think about everything that you want to accomplish in the near future and create an action plan to achieve it. Use the plan of action to guide your to-do list to ensure that you cover everything that is important to you. Don't neglect tasks or errands that will help you achieve your dreams.

GET MORE ORGANIZED

Being organized has the ability to make you feel powerful and in charge, but did you know that it actually does way more than that? Organizing has the ability to reduce stress levels and actually boost your mental health (Safety4sea, 2021). The reason why organizing has such a powerful effect on your mental health is that the opposite is also true. When your life is cluttered, it negatively affects your mental health. The more cluttered and messier your personal space is, the more stress and anxiety it produces. When you take active steps to clean and organize, it gives you control over the mental mess. Cluttered spaces often represent something that is unfinished. It's like leaving a half-baked cake on the counter and trying to move on with your life. Subconsciously, it will occupy your mind and cause stress to build up. According to DR. Mehmet Oz, organizing helps maintain a schedule (Safety4sea, 2021). Another study done by Nicole Keith found that people with clean houses are healthier than people who live messily.

Staying organized isn't just about cleaning your fridge or washing your sheets. You can also organize your mind by removing mental clutter. Here are a couple of tips to stay organized and tackle stress in a helpful manner:

- Use a daily planner.
- Make a weekly and monthly to-do list.
- Keep your space clean and tidy.
- When you feel stressed, take ten minutes to declutter.
- Focus on one task at a time.

- Manage your time.
- Create a routine and stick to it.
- Schedule breaks during the day.
- Start the day with some personal time and take a couple of minutes to be grateful.
- Set goals and track progress.
- Put things away in their right spot so it is easy to find.

Now that you have all the tips you need to stay organized and take back some power from stress, it's time to implement them practically with the following journaling moment. In the next chapter, we'll discover ways to achieve instant relaxation, even in the most stressful situations.

WRITE THE STRESS AWAY

For today's journaling prompt, I want you to take some time and think about the following questions:

1. On a scale of 1 to 10, how would I rate my time management and why?
2. In which areas of my life can my time management improve?
3. What three things can I implement to improve my time management?

4. Which area will I focus on organizing this week, and how do I plan on doing that?

Take your time with these answers and really think about them carefully. Up next, take a look at these checklists that can help you stay organized daily, weekly, and monthly.

Daily Organizing Checklist		
	Mail	• Discard junk mail. • Pay bills immediately to avoid clutter. • File paperwork neatly.
	Keys and personal items	• Put keys in the same spot every day to avoid looking for them when in a hurry. • Designate a drawer or shelf for phones, wallets, sunglasses, etc.
	Housekeeping	• Tidy up the space you occupy before moving on to the next space. • Run the dishwasher at night and empty it first thing in the morning. • Get everything ready for the next morning. • Straighten furniture and throw away trash.

Weekly Organizing Checklist		
	Grocery Shopping and Meal Planning	• Plan out the meals for the week and buy everything in one go. • Shop once a week to avoid unnecessary trips.
	Family Schedules	• Review the schedule for the week and make sure that everyone knows what's happening.
	Laundry	• Set up a laundry schedule. • Do as much laundry, folding, and ironing as possible before the week begins.
	Car	• Remove all the trash. • Remove everything that doesn't belong.

Below, you'll also find a cleaning checklist that you can use to ensure that your house is clean and organized to maximize your time management.

Tidy Up Checklist	
✓	**Kitchen**
	Remove everything that doesn't belong in the kitchen.
	Clean countertops and sink.
	Clean appliances and underneath appliances.
	Clean oven and stove-top.
	Clean the inside and outside of the refrigerator.
	Wash cabinets.
	Tidy up drawers and the pantry.
	Take out the trash.
	Mop.
	Get rid of unused equipment, crockery, and cutlery.
	Get rid of all things that have expired.
	Bedroom
	Remove things that don't belong in this room.
	Donate clothing you don't wear anymore.
	Vacuum closet.
	Dust the dresser and shelves.
	A dust ceiling fan or air-conditioning.
	Clean sheets.

	Bathroom
	Put things back in their place.
	Throw away all empty containers.
	Get rid of all things that have expired.
	Clean the shower and bathtub.
	Wash mirrors.
	Clean the toilet.
	Empty trash.
	Tidy drawers.
	Replace the towels with clean ones.
	Sweep and mop.
	Living Room
	Remove everything that doesn't belong in this room.
	Vacuum.
	Clean couches.
	Remove clutter.
	Dust coffee tables.
	Clean electronics.
	Clean couch covers and cushions.

AN EASY WAY TO REACH OUT A HAND TO SOMEONE ELSE

"No one is useless in this world who lightens the burdens of another."

— *CHARLES DICKENS*

When you're battling with your own stress and anxiety, the last thing you want to do is guide someone else out of the darkness. Indeed, it might feel like an impossible task when you're still working on it yourself.

I've found it helpful to think about Spoon Theory when I've been in this position myself. Spoon Theory was conceptualized by Christine Miserandino and is usually applied to those living with chronic illness. It uses spoons to represent units of energy and explains how these units are depleted, resulting in limited energy to spare. Essentially, each task, no matter how small, uses up a spoon, and with a finite amount of silverware available, these spoons must be used wisely.

This idea can be applied to most areas of life, and as you work on managing your own stress and anxiety, I'd wager that you have a limited amount of spoons for helping other people with theirs.

But when you're starting to see the light at the end of the tunnel and you're learning the very techniques that could help someone else, this can be frustrating… I know because I've been there.

But take heart: There's something you could do right now that will leave your spoons firmly on the table, ready for you to use when you need them. All it takes is a few minutes of your time and a handful of your words.

By leaving a review of this book on Amazon, you'll show other people who are fighting the same battles where they can find the guidance they're looking for.

Simply by letting other readers know how this book has helped you and what they can expect to find inside it, you'll point them in the direction of the guidance that will help them take control of their lives again.

Thank you for your support. Together, we can help each other – and it doesn't have to distract from our own journeys at all.

Scan the QR code below for a quick review!

7

THE RECIPE FOR INSTANT ZEN

A couple of months ago, I had a sudden craving for chocolate cake. I gathered all the ingredients and started making the dessert of my dreams. Three hours later, I was finally done and absolutely exhausted. While I was finally eating my cake, I scrolled past a recipe: Cake in three minutes. I nearly dropped the cake on the floor. Apparently, you can make an instant cake by using the microwave and a certain set of ingredients. I immediately tried it, and it worked! This made me wonder; how often do we seek solutions to our problems that take weeks when there's actually a simple and quick answer in front of us?

Being stressed and anxious is no joke, and it can be very serious, but our minds often make us believe that we need a BIG solution for our stress, which often overwhelms us. In truth, there are many things that you can do to help with the stress that only takes a couple of minutes. In this chapter, we'll look at a multitude of two-minute exercises that can give you instant Zen, no matter the situation. This isn't to say that the three-hour cake didn't work or satisfy my cravings, but in some cases, the microwave cake works just as well.

TWO MINUTES TO CALM

The following tips all take two minutes to accomplish, which means that you can't say that you don't have time to de-stress. If you have more time and feel the need, you can extend your two minutes to five or even ten minutes. Let's take a look at 20 tips to find your calm, which only takes two minutes (Lindberg & Weiss, 2022).

Breathe

Breathing is one of the most effective ways to calm down. The more stressed you get, the shallower your breathing becomes. This sends a message to the brain, which triggers fight or flight mode. When you take slow, deep breaths, you disrupt the loop and send a new message to your brain. Box breathing is a great breathing exercise to start with. Breathe in for four seconds, hold your breath for four seconds, exhale for four seconds, and hold empty for four seconds. Repeat the block and continue for two minutes.

Admit

To release tension and feel less anxious, you need to first admit that you are feeling those things. A lot of the time, we pretend that we're fine and not feeling anxious, when on the inside, it's a different story. The fastest way to feel less stressed is to take a moment and just admit that you are stressed. As soon as you admit it, you'll start to feel the power of stress slip away.

Challenge

We talked about challenging your thoughts in the previous chapter, but if you're feeling stressed and only have two minutes, pause for a second and ask yourself: Is this real? Is this thing I'm stressed about an actual threat? Are the things I fear likely to happen? What is the worst thing that can possibly happen, and how can I handle that? Have I survived worse than this? By challenging your thoughts and answering these questions, you'll start to see that the thing you're stressed about is, in fact, not as big as you thought it to be.

Release

Find a way to release your stress. If it's by screaming, find a pillow and scream into it! If you have more time, do a workout or drink some coffee. Find a way to release the feelings inside of you. I've found that often I feel better just by telling someone what I'm feeling. My friends and I call these *venting moments,* where we can say whatever we want and not be judged for it.

Visualize

Visualizing is a powerful tool for calming yourself down. All you need to do is close your eyes and picture yourself as someone who is extremely calm. See how your body is relaxed, and imagine yourself dealing with whatever is causing you stress without any anxiety. Focus on the calm you're feeling, then open your eyes and move on. By creating a mental picture of what it looks like to be calm, you have a reference for what it would feel like to stay calm, enabling you to do so.

Ask

When you feel anxious, ask yourself, *How important is this really*? If it's not something really important, then you don't have to be stressed about it. You can also ask yourself whether you'll care about this thing in another week or month. If the answer is no, chances are that you don't have to waste any energy being stressed anymore.

Change Focus

When you're too focused on the problem, it's hard to keep calm. So, change your focus for two minutes. Go into a different room, stand outside, or make a cup of coffee. By removing yourself from the problem for two minutes, you'll be able to see the problem from a different perspective and find a new focus when you return to it.

Centering Object

A centering object is something that helps you stay calm and find peace of mind whenever you look at it. For some, it's a stuffed animal or a photo, but it can be anything that reminds you of being calm and breathing deeply. For example, if your wedding ring is your centering object because your spouse brings you peace and a calm mind, take two minutes to look at your ring when you start feeling overwhelmed and anxious.

Relax Your Body

When we're stressed, we tense our bodies. A good way to find your calm is by forcing your body into a relaxed position. Drop your shoulders, straighten your back, smile, or lie down for two minutes. Start with your feet and move up to your head, ensuring that every body part is in a relaxed position.

Pressure Points

Our bodies are full of pressure points that are connected to our nervous systems. When we push down on these pressure points, we start to feel relaxed, and tension gets released. Familiarize yourself with the different pressure points, and take two minutes to press down on these pressure points when you're feeling stressed. One of the most common pressure points is located between your thumb and your index finger, in the nerve that connects the two. Press down for two minutes and feel the tension release.

Fresh Air

If you're feeling tense in your space, perhaps you need some fresh air. Step outside for two minutes and breathe in some fresh air. Removing yourself from the stressful environment and stepping outside can prevent panic attacks, and it can calm down your nervous system almost instantly.

Eat

Fueling your body is an incredibly overlooked step when we get anxious. People tend to go into an extreme mode when anxious: Eating everything they can find or not eating at all. Eating nutritious meals can help you stay calm. A cup of green tea with honey can also help you to reduce stress, as can eating a block of dark chocolate. Above all, eating balanced meals instead of skipping or eating junk food is the best way to take care of your body.

Listen to Music and Dance

Listening to music can instantly release stress. Have a two-minute dance party by cranking up a feel-good song and moving your body. The music will have a calming effect on your mind, and by moving your body, you will release pent-up stress.

Watch a Funny Video

Laughing is a great way to get rid of stress. When you feel anxious and need instant calm, take a couple of minutes and watch a funny video or two. Laughter truly is the best medicine, and it can improve your mood radically.

Write

By now, you know the importance of journaling and writing down your feelings. When feeling stressed, take two minutes and journal what you are feeling and why. As soon as you have it down on paper, you'll feel more relaxed, and it will help you navigate the negative emotions in your mind.

Stress Ball

When you're anxious, interacting with a stress toy can take your mind off the problem and give you a physical outlet for what you're feeling. Try squeezing a stress ball or sculpting something with clay.

Aromatherapy

Aromatherapy is the use of essential oils that help alleviate stress and boost your mood (Lindberg & Weiss, 2022). Common aromas used include

- Bergamot
- Cedarwood
- Chamomile
- Geranium
- Ginger
- Lavender
- Lemon
- Tea tree

Meet Friends

Seeking social support is an extremely effective way of dealing with stress. Whether it's a friend, a colleague, or a family member, reaching out to them can help you feel immediate relief. Take two minutes and give someone a quick call, or walk over to a colleague and have a quick chat.

Pet Your Pet

Spending time with your pet can decrease levels of cortisol and lower your blood pressure. Take two minutes to give Fluffy some love and affection, and you'll feel the tension released almost instantaneously.

Chew Gum

Chewing a piece of gum can reduce anxiety and boost your productivity. If you feel too stressed to concentrate, grab some gum and get chewing!

All of these tips take less than five minutes, but it's completely up to you to implement them. If you leave your anxious thoughts unattended for too long, popping some gum might not help. In the next chapter, we'll talk a bit more about stress-releasing methods that might take a little longer. First, it's time for another journaling moment.

WRITE THE STRESS AWAY

In many cases, the first thing we do as human beings when we feel stressed is to isolate ourselves. We do it as a coping mechanism in a desperate attempt to control our surroundings. The problem is that when we isolate ourselves, we stop other people from helping us. Basically, we cut off our own oxygen supply. Speaking to a friend or a family member when you are stressed is one of the best ways to deal with stress and anxiety. That's why it's so important to know who you can count on and who your support network consists of. The following exercise will help you find your support network so that you know whom to call or reach out to when feeling overwhelmed.

Your Support Network
Who is around you?
Who can you talk to?
How can they help and support you?
How can others tell how you are feeling?
Who else could you look to for support?

8

TRANSFORMING THOUGHTS

The way you think about yourself and talk to yourself can contribute to your stress immensely. Your inner voice can either be your biggest fan or your worst critic. Imagine, for a second, having a best friend who follows you everywhere. Whatever you do, your best friend is cheering you on, wiping away your tears when you're sad, and helping you get up after a fall. It's also your best friend who talks you off the cliff when you feel anxious. It's quite a nice picture to have, right? Now imagine having someone who despises you follow you around. He constantly tears you down, rains on your parade, and convinces you that you're about to fail big-time. It's quite stressful, right? Well, that's exactly how it works with the way we think about ourselves. When we think of ourselves in a positive light, we will succeed and find comfort in ourselves. When we have constant negative and limited thoughts about ourselves, however, we will most definitely feel anxious and stressed.

Negative self-talk can take many forms. Sometimes it hides behind constructive criticism, while other times, it's downright bullying (Scott, 2022). It's basically an inner dialogue that you cultivate about where you limit your potential and what you believe you are capable of. Negative self-talk can take the form of filtering, personalizing, catastrophizing, and polarizing. It's important to be aware of your negative self-talk in order to change the narrative and transform the way you think about yourself.

In this chapter, we'll talk all about transforming thoughts from being negative and limiting to being uplifting and positive. We'll look at the side effects of negative self-talk, what limiting beliefs are, and how to change the way we talk to ourselves.

THE DANGERS OF NEGATIVE SELF-TALK

Negative self-talk can be very damaging to your mental and physical well-being. A study found that self-blame and negative self-talk can increase the risk of depression and other mental health problems (Scott, 2022).

When you're constantly bombarded with negative self-talk, and focus on negativity, you will experience decreased motivation and productivity. However, the consequences of negative self-talk go beyond the idea of losing productivity. It can lead to pretty serious problems and can be extremely dangerous.

Let's have a look at four dangers of negative self-talk (Scott, 2022):

- **Limited thinking**: If you tell yourself that you can't do something, chances are that you can't and that you never will be able to. The more you believe in yourself, the faster you'll achieve your goals and experience less stress.
- **Perfectionism**: Being a perfectionist is extremely damaging to your self-confidence. The more of a perfectionist you are, the more you'll feel depressed and stressed about everything that you do. Negative self-talk will constantly remind you that you are not perfect, which might cause a spiral.
- **Feelings of depression**: Negative self-talk can lead to depression, which, if left unchecked, can be extremely dangerous and damaging.
- **Relationship challenges**: When you are constantly negative, you will become insecure and needy. This will push other people away

since negativity is not something that you can hide.

Now, as much as I want to dive deep into each of these dangers, I would like to focus on one that I believe most people struggle with unknowingly, and that is limiting beliefs.

LIMITING BELIEFS

Limiting beliefs are assumptions or perceptions that you have about yourself and about how you fit into the world (Blackman, 2018). These assumptions are called limiting beliefs because they are holding you back in some way or another. Having limiting beliefs stops you from achieving what you are truly capable of, and you settle for what you think is achievable for you.

Let's have a look at a couple of examples of limiting beliefs (101 Planners, 2021):

- I'm not good enough.
- I'm not smart enough.
- I will always fail.
- Bad things always happen to me.
- I don't deserve success.
- I'm unlovable.
- Things will always be hard for me.

- All rich people are greedy.
- No one cares about me.
- I'll be happy as soon as I change.

Having limiting beliefs doesn't just stop you from living your best life and achieving greatness; it also contributes to your stress levels. When you have an accurate belief system about how the world works, you are prepared to some extent for whatever happens. A good understanding and belief system will help you to not feel as stressed about life because, most of the time, things happen the way that you expect. When you have limiting beliefs, you do not have an accurate understanding of yourself, the world, or the people around you, leaving you unprepared and vulnerable to misinterpretation (MentalHelp, n.d.). So, if limiting beliefs are unhealthy for our mental health, then why do so many people struggle with them? To answer that question, we need to take a look at the causes of limiting beliefs and how to overcome them.

CAUSES FOR LIMITING BELIEFS

Limiting beliefs start in childhood and are generally caused by a negative experience that leaves an imprint on our subconscious mind. These false beliefs or stories become embedded when the experience is repeated or when you were very young when it happened. When you adopt a limiting belief as a child, it will become part of your survival mechanism as an adult. For example, if someone told you that you, as a young child, were stupid, you believe that you are not intelligent enough for certain career paths, so you choose a career path that is considered easy and safe.

Overcoming limiting beliefs is not easy, but it's not impossible. For a very long time, I believed that I was not a good father, which, surprisingly, is what made me an inadequate father. My beliefs formed my actions, which ended up with the results I expected. When I changed my limiting beliefs, I experienced the joys of fatherhood and was able to be a better father to my children. So, how do we overcome our limiting beliefs? Step-by-step.

OVERCOMING LIMITING BELIEFS

Before we look at ways of overcoming limiting beliefs, I want you to take a second and let the following sink in: Don't expect change overnight. Limiting beliefs form over many years, and you can't expect them to go away after one meditation session. It will require many hours of input and challenging your beliefs, but it will be worth it, and you will get there. That being said, let's look at five ways to overcome limiting beliefs.

Reframing

If you're able to recognize your limiting belief, reframing is a great way to overcome it. Once you recognize your limiting belief, you can actively decide to reject it and reframe it into a positive belief. Basically, you replace your limiting belief with one that empowers and encourages you.

There are four steps to reframing (101 Planners, 2021):

1. Recognize the limiting belief.
2. Reject it.
3. Reframe it into a positive empowering belief.
4. Write down 3–4 statements that support the new belief.

Alternative Beliefs

Most of the time, there are other explanations that you didn't consider before adopting the limiting belief that you have. Think about the example we spoke about earlier regarding being told you were stupid as a child. Instead of accepting that as the truth, an alternative explanation could have been that the one who told you that you were stupid was envious of your intelligence or that he/she was hurt and didn't mean it. Creating alternative beliefs will help you realize that perhaps what you believe isn't true.

1. Start by asking yourself. "What if I'm wrong?" Think of alternative reasons and uncover why you believe this limiting belief.
2. Next, ask yourself, "How is this serving me?" If the thought isn't serving you in a positive way, let it go.

Hypnosis

Hypnosis can help you understand why you developed the limiting belief, and it will provide you with a pattern. If you're not comfortable with hiring a hypnotherapist, there are numerous resources and books that can teach you how to use self-hypnosis to overcome limiting thoughts (101 Planners, 2021).

Positive Affirmations

Positive affirmations are a brilliant way of improving your self-image and self-esteem. When you create your own affirmations, you make a personal statement about yourself that is positive that you can tell yourself throughout the day instead of listening to your inner critic and hating yourself.

Here are some examples of affirmations:

- I deserve to be happy.
- The more I give, the more I will receive.

- I am letting go of negativity and embracing positive energy.
- I will be a success, and I will be generous with my money.
- I am an excellent employee.
- I am a great parent.

Burn Them

Start by making a list of all the limiting beliefs you have that are preventing you from living your best life. Next, list the negative messages that you tell your body and mind about your abilities and your future. Take some time to apologize to yourself and promise yourself that you will change and be kinder to your body, mind, and spirit. Take the list of limiting beliefs and negative emotions and destroy it. You can either burn it or shred it, whatever works for you. As you destroy the list, breathe deeply and allow your mind to release the negative thoughts (101 Planners, 2021).

LEARNING POSITIVE SELF-TALK

A big part of overcoming limiting beliefs and reframing your thoughts is by practicing positive self-talk (Estrada, 2020). Positive self-talk is speaking kindly to yourself and treating your mind and body with compassion. It's when you treat yourself the way you would treat your best friend. Positive self-talk helps you gain a new perspective on life and improves your relationships. It also increases your self-confidence and decreases your loneliness. As important as self-talk is, it can be tricky to know where to start. It might even feel awkward to show yourself some kindness after years of entertaining your inner critic, but with the right practices, you'll be adding positive self-talk to your daily routine in no time. Here are three ways that you can implement positive self-talk daily.

Make it Feel True

When positive self-talk feels forced, it can push us in the opposite direction from where we want to go. For example, if you want to start speaking positivity over your mental capacity but feel like you have a mental block, it might be ineffective to look in the mirror and fake a smile. Instead, be honest with yourself. Instead of saying, "I am super smart," try something like, "Despite my feelings, I know that I am adequate." The more honest you are, the less resistance you'll experience (Estrada, 2020).

Change Behavior

When you engage in behavior that confirms your limiting beliefs or negative self-talk, it won't be as effective as when you simply say something positive.

You need to back up your positive statements with some action (Estrada, 2020). Ask yourself, "What can I do to prove that this positive statement is true?" When you act on the positive statement, it will become easier and easier to continue the positive self-talk.

Start in One Area

Starting with one area and working your way up to the others is a great way to begin. Just like any new habit, starting small will eventually take you further than jumping into the deep end. If you struggle with positive self-talk regarding your work, start there. Once you've got that under control, include another area (Estrada, 2020).

Transforming your thoughts can make a massive difference in the state of your mental well-being and your emotions. In the next chapter, we'll talk about emotional regulation and how we can deal with it, but first, it's time to journal a little bit.

WRITE THE STRESS AWAY

For this chapter's journaling section, I want you to be honest and open with yourself. Below you'll find 20 questions that require answering. Fill in the blank spaces to discover how you are feeling about yourself at this stage in your life, which will give away a lot regarding the state of your inner dialogue. Take at least 30 minutes to carefully work through these questions and answer them with vulnerability. Answering these questions will give you insight into what makes you happy and how you currently treat yourself.

1. What have I always wanted to do?
2. What am I secretly afraid of?
3. What would I enjoy doing this week?
4. What do I often look forward to?
5. What do I feel my future might hold for me?
6. Where do I get my strength from?
7. Who can't I live without?
8. What would I never do in my life?
9. When do I feel at my best?
10. What do I love most in this world?
11. What do I find hard to do?
12. What is my hope for my future?
13. What makes me extremely angry?
14. What do I fear the most?
15. What are my thoughts on this week?
16. What do I deeply desire?
17. When do I flourish and thrive?
18. What do I often think about in secret?
19. What do I find hard to admit?
20. What do I regret not doing?

9

REGULATING THE EMOTIONAL UPHEAVAL

Being stressed comes with a lot of emotions. Have you ever been so stressed that you just want to punch something, and then five minutes later, you're bawling your eyes out? Well, that's not as strange as you might think. Prolonged stress can lead to something called emotional dysregulation, also known as mood swings. Emotional dysregulation is an emotional response that is poorly regulated and doesn't quite fall in your normal range of emotions (Sachdev, 2021). When you experience emotional dysregulation, you might have anger outbursts, anxiety, depression, and self-damaging behavior. Emotional dysregulation can be caused by various things, like childhood trauma, neglect, or a traumatic injury. When left unchecked, it can lead to serious problems, and in general, it leads to a lot of stress. When you feel like you're not in control of your emotions, it's hard to relax because you are constantly scared of yourself. Imagine having a roommate who is always unstable, gets angry quickly, and often threatens your life. Would you be able to relax, or would you constantly fear her arrival? That's exactly how it feels for someone who struggles with emotional dysregulation.

If you experience emotional dysregulation to extreme measures, I'll advise you to talk to a healthcare professional. There are many medical treatments that can help, and they might lead to a diagnosis that can help you cope with your emotions. However, if you're experiencing emotional dysregulation because of stress in your life, this chapter will help you identify the unhealthy ways you are currently dealing with your emotions, as well as provide tools and skills that you can implement to help you manage your emotions better. If, at any point during this chapter, you feel like your emotional dysregulation isn't normal, I really want to encourage you to take a moment, breathe deeply, and consider talking to someone about it. Emotional dysregulation can be quite dangerous if left unchecked, so let's rather play it safe. Let's start by looking at ways emotions are being mismanaged.

EMOTIONAL MISMANAGEMENT

We all deal with our emotions differently. Emotional management is how you personally deal with emotions that are overwhelming and out of place. It includes skills and tools that you've learned during your lifetime that you use to manage what you are feeling. The problem is that many of us mismanage our emotions because we never learned how to deal with them properly. So, we rely on unhealthy methods to make us feel okay, which work at the moment but have serious long-term effects. According to the team at Mental Health America, there are five harmful ways that people tend to lean towards when they mismanage their emotions. Let's take a quick look at these five emotional mismanagement tools (Mental Health America, 2019).

Denial

When a person refuses to accept that something is wrong, it's called denial. This might also happen when someone suggests you get help for your emotional outburst, and you get offensive, claiming that nothing is wrong. For a very long time, I struggled with denial. So many people that I love have tried to make me aware that I have a problem with stress, yet I would always deny it and say that I was perfectly fine. Well, I definitely wasn't perfectly fine, and if only I had listened earlier, I might have saved a lot of people a lot of pain. The reason why denial is problematic is that the emotions you're denying having are getting bottled up, and pretty soon, they will explode.

Withdrawal

Withdrawal and spending some time alone are not the same. Wanting some alone time is perfectly normal and quite good for you, but when you start to withdraw from social events or simply from talking to other people because you don't have the energy for it, you should see it as a warning sign. I started withdrawing when I felt ashamed of my behavior. I remember having an emotional outburst in front of my family, and immediately regretting it, feeling exposed and out of control. So, I withdrew and kept to myself, scared of my own emotions. The problem is that we need to interact with other people in order to be balanced and healthy.

Bullying

When we hear the word *bully,* we usually think of schoolyard drama and shoving others into lockers, and yes, that is also bullying. However, as adults, we can sometimes bully others without knowing it. I used to bully my family whenever I felt bad about myself, picking out their flaws or bringing up things in conversation that I knew they didn't enjoy. Making someone feel bad about themselves is a very unhealthy coping mechanism, and it's often those closest to us that get the worst of it. Using your friends and family as a punching bag might be tempting, but it doesn't deal with the underlying stress and will ultimately only make you feel even worse about yourself.

Self-Harm

Self-harm can take many forms, from cutting to starving to putting yourself in dangerous situations. Many people practice self-harm as a way of dealing with their emotions because then they feel like they have control over their pain. It might provide temporary relief and power, but it can become very addictive and lead to a lot of pain and damage. Using self-harm as a coping mechanism for your emotions never works because you'll end up feeling more out of control than before.

Substance Use

Using alcohol or drugs to numb your emotions is a very popular way of dealing with unwanted emotions, especially among adults. Substances numb your emotions, which is why so many people grab the bottle when stressed. The problem is that once the alcohol works itself out, the same stress will still be there. It doesn't fix the problem, and it can often make your emotions even more uncontrollable, leading to periods of crying or angry outbursts.

Now that we've looked at the unhealthy way that we tend to cope with unwanted emotions, it's time to take a look at how we should deal with our emotions instead. All of the above methods lead to you hating your own emotions, which is not the point of emotion management. Self-regulation is all about loving yourself enough to take care of your emotions properly.

SELF-REGULATION

Self-regulation is the ability to control your emotions and behavior in a way that is healthy. Self-regulation does not mean hiding away from your feelings or acting cold; it means acknowledging and dealing with your emotions in a way that contributes to your long-term goals. For example, let's say you have a goal to get promoted at work. If your boss does something that upsets you, freaking out and fighting with him won't help, but neither will saying nothing. Self-regulation will help you to control your emotions at the moment and then address your issues in a way that is professional and respectful. Self-regulation involves the ability to rebound from disappointment and act in a way that is consistent (Cuncic, 2022). Being able to self-regulate is an incredibly important skill in emotional intelligence.

When we talk about self-regulation, it can mean one of two things: Emotional self-regulation or behavioral self-regulation. Let's take a quick look at what they entail.

- Behavioral self-regulation is the ability to act in your long-term best interest. It allows you to feel one way but act in another. It's like going to work, despite really not wanting to.
- Emotional self-regulation involves controlling your emotions in a way that is healthy. It includes calming yourself down when angry or putting your bad mood aside to make the most out of the day.

In order to understand self-regulation, we need to take a closer look at what is called the "Self-Regulation Theory" (Cuncic, 2022).

Self-Regulation Theory

Self-regulation theory (SRT) outlines the process and components required when taking control of your emotions or behavior. There are four components involved with the self-regulation theory:

1. Your standards of desirable behavior.
2. The motivation to meet these standards.
3. Monitoring situations and patterns.
4. Using willpower and inner strength to not act on impulse.

These four components interact with one another to determine self-regulation. In order to self-regulate, you first need to identify the behavior and emotion that you would like to display. How would you like to be perceived by others? By identifying your desired behavior, the next steps can fall into place. However, self-regulation is a bit more complicated than that and is actually part of a psychological model (Ackerman, 2019).

The Psychology of Self-Regulation

Self-regulation is a continuous process. It's not something you do once and then happens naturally. It takes a lot of practice, awareness, and activity. Self-regulation requires three constant actions from you:

1. Monitoring your own behavior.
2. Judging your behavior.
3. Reacting to your behavior.

When you behave in a way that is not desirable, you will only be able to identify it as undesirable by monitoring your own behavior. Once you're monitored, you can judge it and ask yourself why it was or was not desirable. Then, you can react to your behavior by either apologizing, taking active steps to be better at it, or, if you choose to react poorly, creating more undesirable outcomes (Ackerman, 2019).

Self-regulation is not the same as self-control, although they might sound the same at first. Self-control is about inhabiting strong impulses, while self-regulation is about reducing the frequency of the impulses. In fact, self-regulation makes self-control possible. Self-regulation can be viewed as a more automatic process, while self-control is a decision at the moment.

Examples of Self-Regulation

- A nurse who remains calm when a patient is angry about something that she has no control over.
- A teenager refrains from slamming his bedroom door after his mom tells him that he can't go to the party he wanted to.
- A couple who are in the midst of an argument decides to take some time to cool off and think

about everything before continuing the conversation.

- A young man who just started working decides to go home early instead of hitting the clubs with his buddies because he has to work the next day.
- A mother-in-law refrains from telling her daughter-in-law how to raise her children because she knows there are some things every parent needs to discover for themselves.

Self-regulation is incredibly important for your mental well-being. People who are able to self-regulate actively are more likely to enjoy their lives and feel less stressed about things that are out of their control. That being said, let's take a look at some self-regulation strategies that we all can practice in order to reduce stress.

SELF-REGULATION TOOLS

Self-regulation is not an easy task, but the more you practice it, the more natural it will become. Self-regulation is the art of pausing between feelings and reactions (Chowdhury, 2019). It helps us slow down and objectively evaluate the state of things and the nature of our feelings. Cultivating self-regulation is not impossible, and every person is capable of self-regulating their emotions and behaviors. Let's take a look at a couple of tools that you can use to help you with self-regulation.

Cognitive Reappraisal

Cognitive reappraisal is when we alter the way we think. It improves your mental flexibility and acceptance greatly, which helps you to manage your emotions and behavior better. Cognitive reappraisal skills include visualization practices and thought replacement. In action, cognitive reappraisal will look like this:

Situation: Your boss appears angry because of something you did.

Old thinking: "I'm getting fired. I'm not needed anymore. I only make a mess of things."

New thinking: "I can make this up. My boss is angry now, but he will calm down and see all the good things I've done."

Mindfulness

Mindfulness practices are great self-regulation tools. Mindfulness makes you aware of your actions and emotions, and it helps you identify all aspects of the situation. Doing breathing exercises or practicing a sensory relaxation method can help you calm the storm inside of you and provide you with a way out.

Seeking Help

In many cases, the most effective way of dealing with severe emotional mismanagement is by seeking help. There is absolutely no shame in seeking help when struggling, whether mentally, emotionally, or physically. Professionals can help you deal with anger issues, outbursts, and other emotional mismanagement issues. Seeking help is highly encouraged, especially if you feel like you're trying your best but making no progress at all.

Six-Second Pause

A six-second pause method is a self-regulation tool that you can use to gain self-control during an emotionally-charged situation (Goalbook, 2022). This strategy involves creating a moment to force your brain to put your emotions aside and engage the thinking part of the brain, forming a constructive response instead of an emotional one. Take six seconds to think about something else; for example, name six of your favorite foods or six of your dearest friends whom you love. By thinking about something and listing six things, you activate the thinking part of your brain, which overrides the emotional part for the time being (Goalbook, 2022).

The Eight Cs

The eight Cs are a method of creating time and space in your day for these eight things. According to specialists, when you incorporate these eight things into your daily life, you will gain more perspective, awareness, and control over your emotions and behaviors while also de-stressing at the same time. To be the best version of yourself, you need to find time to get to know your true self. These eight things will help you do just that and regulate your emotions at the same time.

The eight Cs include

- Compassion
- Creativity
- Connection
- Curiosity
- Clarity
- Confidence
- Calm
- Courage

STOPP Strategy

STOPP strategy can guide you to calm in the midst of emotions. It makes use of Cognitive Behavioral Therapy (CBT) and meditation to more effectively address and manage your emotions. The following table will describe the steps of STOPP in a practical way. I want to encourage you to try it the next time you feel unnerved or emotional in conversation.

Letter	What it stands for	Description
S	Stop!	Pause for a moment before you respond or react.
T	Take a breath	Take note of your breathing. Do a quick breathing exercise to calm your breathing.
O	Observe	Ask yourself: - What thoughts am I entertaining right now? - Where is my focus? - What am I reacting to?
P	Pull Back	Ask yourself: - What is the bigger picture? - Can I look at this from a different perspective? - Is this a thought, fact, or opinion?
P	Proceed	- What is the best way to proceed? - What can I do to fit with my values? - What will be effective?

Any one of these incredible self-regulation tools can help you with behavior and emotions. Ultimately, success depends on you. How much effort you put into these tools and how effectively you use them will determine how effectively you manage your stress and regulate your emotions.

EMOTIONAL REGULATION SKILLS

Tools are something that you keep in your pocket and get out whenever you need them. It's something that you do in the heat of the moment that guides you through calming down and releasing stress. On the other hand, skills require some learning and implementation on a daily basis so that they can eventually come naturally and be a part of who you are. We've already discussed a few self-regulation tools that you can use when necessary, but now it's time to look at some emotional regulation skills that you can teach yourself until it becomes your natural response subconsciously. Let's take a look at ten emotional regulation skills that every adult should have (Invah, 2015). This can be used as a measurement to see whether you need to put in some extra effort to obtain emotional regulation skills. Give yourself a point for every skill below that you do have and use that as a measurement.

✓	**Emotional Regulation Skill**
	I am capable of identifying my own emotions and not getting confused by what I'm feeling.
	I am capable of identifying other people's emotions and don't just label everyone as "having a bad mood."
	I can start and pursue goals without feeling stressed or anxious.
	I can tolerate awkwardness in conversation.
	I am capable of having deep and intimate conversations with others.
	I can stand my ground and don't crumble when I'm under pressure.
	I can soothe myself and my emotions.
	I can soothe other people's emotions.
	I am good at waiting and don't feel rushed to finish everything today.
	I am capable of managing my own positive emotions.

Now that you know what your emotional regulation level is, use it as a guide and implement some of the above self-regulation tools to improve your emotional self-regulation. Having personal time is a wonderful way of dealing with emotions, which is why we'll talk all about self-care in the next chapter. First, let's journal the stress away for a bit.

WRITE THE STRESS AWAY

When emotions are mismanaged, we might experience something called an *emotional leak.* Emotional leakage occurs when you bottle up your emotions without managing them properly, causing them to spill over in an undesired way. Have you ever experienced an emotional leak before? Take a couple of minutes and journal on this.

The *PLEASE* method is a wonderful way to make sure that you take good care of your body, mind, and soul. When you take care of *PLEASE,* you are more likely to experience good emotional regulation. Take a couple of minutes and go through the steps of the *PLEASE* method.

PLEASE		
PL	Treating **P**hysical **Il**lness	Don't ignore any physical discomfort you might have. Get it checked out, and take good care of your health.
E	**E**ating Healthy	Have balanced meals, and make sure that you include enough nutrients in your diet.
A	**A**voiding mood-altering drugs	Stay away from using drugs and alcohol as a means of coping.
S	**S**leeping well	Get at least eight hours of sleep to ensure that you are energized.
E	**E**xercising	Exercise regularly to take care of your body and mind.

10

SELF-CARE SOLUTION

It can be incredibly difficult to make time for self-care. So often, taking care of ourselves takes a back seat when our calendar fills up or our days spin out of control. It's important to remember that self-care is not selfish; it is a sense of self-compassion that we all need in order to function positively. When we are kind to ourselves, we'll want to improve for the better. When we are constantly tearing ourselves down, we'll get stuck in a mindset of negativity and stress. Self-compassion helps us to release stress from our lives by removing the fear of making a mistake. When you are self-compassionate, you motivate yourself to be a better you in a way that is healthy and fruitful. Many studies show that people who are self-compassionate are less depressed and anxious (Neff, 2011). When you are able to be self-compassionate with yourself, you are less likely to get anxious over work and other performance-driven anxieties.

That's why this chapter is all about self-compassion and self-care. We'll first take a look at self-compassion, what it is and how to grow self-compassion oneself. Then, we'll look at self-care and various strategies that we can implement to practice self-care on a daily basis. Let's get right into it.

WHAT IS SELF-COMPASSION

The problem with self-compassion is that many people don't understand its full meaning or what it entails. We think that if we don't harm ourselves, we are being self-compassionate when in truth, it requires much more than just that. There are many misconceptions regarding self-compassion, including the idea that it is selfish and a form of self-pity. Self-compassion is definitely not a form of self-pity but actually an antidote to self-pity. When you feel sorry for yourself, you don't seek a way out of your situation. With self-compassion, you are more likely to accept what happened and find a way to move forward and improve while being kind to yourself. Self-compassion is also not a sign of weakness; it takes incredible strength to be kind to yourself and to love yourself regardless of your flaws and mistakes (Neff, 2015).

Self-compassion involves treating yourself the way you would treat others when they are struggling. It requires you to motivate yourself, even when you've failed; to love yourself, even when you feel unworthy; to keep going, even when it's easier to give up. Self-compassion is not something that comes naturally to all of us, especially when you struggle with perfectionism. Luckily, it is something that can be taught. Let's take a look at a couple of strategies we can use to grow self-compassion.

STRATEGIES TO GROW SELF-COMPASSION

Self-compassion doesn't develop overnight. It's more like a habit, where you need to build it from the ground up until it becomes natural. In the modern day, we are bombarded with so many messages about *being better* and changing ourselves to fit the mold that it's no wonder we don't like ourselves very much. It's up to you to change that thinking and change your judgment to kindness. The following four strategies can help you grow your self-compassion so that you can be kind to yourself and reap the benefits of it.

Write About It

Journaling and writing down your feelings are like water for a newly planted seed. When you write in your journal on a daily basis, self-compassion will grow and cover your battered heart from years of the inner critic being in charge. Prioritize putting your thoughts and feelings on paper. Many of us stay away from journaling because we feel like we're not good at it or because we think it's just not for us. However, journaling is not about being good at writing, it's beneficial to everyone. When you put your feelings on paper, your thoughts become more than just a weightless sentence swirling in your head. Instead, they gain substance, take from it, and live in reality. When your feelings and thoughts become real, you can face them and cultivate self-compassion.

Talk About It

If writing about your feelings is like water, talking about them is fertilizer. Talking about your feelings and thoughts can help you feel validated when they're shared with the right person. People who don't have your best interest at heart or people who are toxic might use your vulnerabilities against you and manipulate you into believing something about yourself that is not true. When you share your feelings with a good friend, they can help you understand that this thought or feeling doesn't make you a terrible person; it's completely human. Sharing with a friend can remove the weight off your chest and experience relief.

Observe Yourself

One of the best ways to cultivate self-compassion is to observe how you speak to yourself versus how you speak about a friend. How do you observe others who are struggling and talking negatively about themselves? Do you feel compassion towards them? Chances are, you'll feel compassion for them and try to convince them that they are not terrible or a failure. Now observe how you view yourself in the same situation. Are you less compassionate with yourself than with others? Allow our feelings to flow and stop fighting the content that comes with them. Move toward acceptance so that you can have a safe relationship with yourself.

Unplug

Quiet time cultivates deeper emotions and self-discovery. When you unplug from all your gadgets and enjoy a cup of coffee on the balcony, you create a moment of peace and quiet, which is what your soul needs. Take some time to get into nature, away from the humdrum of bustling life, and allow your senses to experience the world around you. When you experience life, you come to terms with a lot of things and gain new perspectives, growing in self-compassion in the process.

Above all, self-compassion grows out of self-care, and self-care grows out of self-compassion. These two concepts are like two sides of the same coin. Let's take a closer look at what self-care is and how you can cultivate self-care at home.

SELF-CARE

Self-care means taking care of yourself in order to be healthy in all areas of your life. Self-care is part of the solution to fighting stress, anxiety, and even burnout (Lawler, 2021). It is not selfish or self-indulgent but rather a symptom of self-compassion and self-love.

You need self-care in every area of your life, including:

- Mental self-care
- Physical self-care
- Emotional self-care
- Financial self-care
- Environmental self-care

When you practice self-care, you take care of all the above areas in various ways to ensure that you are as healthy and happy as you can be. When you are struggling with burnout, self-care can help you heal and focus on your daily needs. You actively take action to rest and recover, which is the only way to approach burnout. You can't bulldoze through burnout or work it away. Trust me; it will only get worse. When you have self-care practices in place, you will recognize signs of distress in the different areas of your life before they become a bigger problem. You'll be aware of your thoughts, feelings, and physical well-being. Self-care alone can't solve your burnout, anxiety, or depression, but it will guide you to the best practices to deal with it, whether it be taking time off or speaking to a professional.

AT-HOME SELF-CARE STRATEGIES

While some self-care strategies involve going away for the weekend or taking a trip to the spa, real self-care happens every day in the little things. Self-care doesn't have to be fancy or complicated. In fact, self-care is most effective when done on a daily basis in everything that you do.

Here are a few ideas for at-home self-care (Triangle Family Dental, 2020):

- Take a break from the news and leave space for some positivity.

- Get moving with light exercises like yoga or walking.
- Relax with an activity that you enjoy, like coloring, building a puzzle, or playing a family game.
- Talk to others about your concerns instead of bottling it all up.
- Take care of your body and pay attention to what it needs and requires, whether rest or activity.
- Socialize with other people to de-stress and grow your circle of interest. Isolation is not always the answer when you need self-care.
- Meditate and take care of your spiritual well-being.
- Spend more time with your pets and relax by doing an activity that involves them.
- Keep a gratitude journal and write down everything that you are grateful for every day.
- Wash your hair and take a bubble bath.
- Dedicate time to work on your personal goals and to dream about the future.
- Clean out a space that's been bothering you.

As you can see, self-care isn't as glamorous or pretty as some marketing materials make it look. It sometimes requires some ugly tears and true self-awareness, but it's always kind and compassionate. In the next chapter, we'll look at an important aspect of self-care and self-compassion, and that is our sleep hygiene. For now, let's practice some self-care and journal the stress away with the following activity.

WRITE THE STRESS AWAY

For today's journaling activity, you're going to create your own self-care routine. Below, you'll find a template that you can use to create your own self-care checklist. All of the actions and activities mentioned below should be included in your daily routine, no matter how small. For example, social activity can be checking in with a friend or talking to your kids after dinner. Make the checklist as personal as possible to ensure that you get the most out of it.

Daily Self-Care Checklist	
	Follow a morning routine.
	An activity to help physical wellness.
	An action to take care of intellectual wellness.
	Spiritual wellness activity.
	Action to promote emotional wellness.
	Social activity.
	Something to improve your environment.
	Take care of financial tasks.
	Follow an evening routine.
	Think of ways to improve tomorrow's wellness.
	Rest.
	Do Something that makes you smile.

11

THE BALANCE BETWEEN MOVEMENT AND REST

Over the years, I've found that there are two things that get thrown out of the window as soon as I get stressed: exercise and sleep. When I'm stressed, I stop exercising because I get consumed with work. I refuse to take a couple of minutes to clear my head and exercise because I'm convinced that the work I'm dealing with is more important than my health. Secondly, I stopped going to bed at a decent time of the night, and I woke up at crazy hours, convinced that then I'll be able to do more. In reality, I'm just prolonging my anxiety and stress by removing two of the best methods of dealing with stress. I once read a quote that said, "You're one workout away from a good mood," and it annoyed me so much that I decided to give it a try. Much to my disappointment, it actually worked! But there's a balance that needs to be maintained between movement and rest in order to battle stress effectively.

In this chapter, we'll talk about how both exercise and sleep can combat stress, and we'll discover practical ways in which we can use both of these activities to get rid of anxiety and stress. Let's start by looking at how exercise combats stress.

EXERCISE AND STRESS

We all know that exercise is important for taking care of our physical bodies, but we often fail to recognize the impact that exercise can have on our mental health. When you exercise, you boost your endorphins, also known as your happy hormones. Endorphins don't just make you feel happy and chirpy, though; they actively combat cortisol, which is the stress hormone in our body. When you move your body, you take care of your mental well-being, and it can reduce anxiety and stress. Different exercises can make you feel different ways, but they all leave you with positive change, even though it might not feel like it during the exercise. Exercises such as high-intensity workouts can even improve your mental strength, making you less vulnerable to mental illness and stress (Livingston, 2022). When you make exercise part of your stress combating plan, you'll feel more energized and less anxious on a daily basis. This doesn't mean that you have to turn into a gym junkie and exercise seven days a week for hours on end. Even a brisk walk can help fight the stress in your body. Let's take a look at some of the best exercises to beat stress.

EXERCISES TO BEAT STRESS

There's no wrong exercise when we look at ways to remove stress. No matter what kind of movement you do, it will contribute positively to your stress levels. If you have no idea where to start, look at the table below for some exercises that you can do and an explanation as to why they're great.

Exercise	Explanation
Brisk Walk	A 10-minute walk can be enough to restore your calm, but if you're extremely stressed, try walking for 45 minutes.
Jogging	When you run, you release even more happy hormones than when you are walking. Make sure that you run in cushioned shoes to ensure support and comfort.
Swimming	Swimming is a great full-body workout, and it doubles as resistance training. When you are submerged in water, it is very soothing for your anxiety and stress.
Cycling	Cycling is easy on the joints, and it raises your heart rate. When you cycle for 30 minutes, you can completely restore your calm.
Dancing	Put on some music and bust a move! When you dance, you get a workout while relaxing and removing feelings of anxiety.
Boxing	Boxing is a great way to get rid of frustration and anger. It's a great way of reducing stress in a way that also gets your blood pumping.
HIIT Workout	High-intensity interval training is a great way to burn a lot of stress, and it will leave you feeling strong and powerful afterwards.

SLEEP STRESS AWAY

When you lose sleep, you activate a region of the brain that controls worry and emotional processing, meaning that if you don't sleep properly, you might experience anxiety and stress because of it (Banner Health, 2019). A lack of good sleep overworks the heart, which also causes stress and negatively influences your mental well-being. That's why it's important to maintain a good sleep pattern and practice good sleep hygiene. If you wake up feeling more tired than you did before bed, your sleep hygiene might not be great. The following tips are simple tips that you can implement to improve the quality of sleep and reduce stress. All of these are easy and practical and only require a little bit of attention and a change in your routine (Mawer, 2020).

Seven Tips to Better Your Sleep

1. Don't consume coffee late in the day. Try to cut yourself off from all caffeine by 4 p.m. Even if you think it doesn't affect you, it influences the depth of your sleep. It might not keep you awake, but it will prevent you from going into a deep sleep.
2. Reduce naps during the day. If you're really exhausted and can't stay awake, limit yourself

to 20 minutes. Irregular naps during the day can lead to struggling to fall asleep at night.

3. Don't drink alcohol close to bedtime. Alcohol influences your sleep hormones negatively and can increase the symptoms of sleep apnea, snoring, and disrupted sleep.
4. Set your bedroom temperature. When your room is too hot or too cold, you'll struggle to fall and stay asleep. If your bedroom is too hot, it will prevent you from going into a state of deep sleep, and it can increase wakefulness.
5. Don't eat too late in the evening. When you eat too late, your body will stay awake to process the food instead of sleeping. Try to stay away from late-night snacks and make sure you eat at least four hours before bed.
6. Take a relaxing bath or shower before bed. Studies show that when you sleep before bed, you improve your quality of sleep significantly, and you'll get more deep sleep.
7. Get a comfortable bed and sheets that your skin enjoys. Don't cut the budget on your bed. It is literally the furniture that you will use the most, so invest in a good mattress. Having sheets with a nice texture also contributes to sleep quality.

With exercise and sleep, you can combat a good amount of stress, but you have to be committed to ensuring you have good sleep hygiene and get enough movement. In the next chapter, we'll look at how different breathing techniques can help with stress relief and recovery.

WRITE THE STRESS AWAY

Having good sleep hygiene is incredibly important to battling stress, so for today's journaling moment, you'll be assessing the state of your sleep patterns. Below you'll see a table with a question, a reason, and space for your action plan. Read the question carefully, then the reason, and then think of a way in which you can improve on the answer to your question by implementing healthy sleep patterns. The idea is to not just come up with an action plan but to actually implement it throughout your week.

The Question	The Reason	My Action Plan
Is it dark enough?	The darker the room, the better for your sleep.	(Example: I will get blackout curtains.)
Is it cool enough?	Maintain a temperature of 60–65 °F.	
Is the room tidy?	A tidy room contributes to better sleep.	
Did I stop using my phone and other electronics long before bedtime?	Using LED displays in bed near bedtime impacts sleep negatively.	
Do I use my bedroom to eat and work?	When you use your bedroom as other spaces, your mind won't be aware that it's the sleep space, preventing you from feeling sleepy.	
Does my bedroom feel peaceful?	Decorate your bedroom in a way that makes you feel peaceful.	
Does my room look relaxing?	Bright and shocking colors might not make you feel ready for bed.	
How does my room smell?	Pleasant, calming smells can help you drift off.	
Is my room sleep-friendly?	Your room should feel like somewhere you can escape from your busy day.	

12

BREATHING TECHNIQUES AND RECOVERY

Breathing is something that we don't often think about; it just happens naturally. Unfortunately, this means that we often forget to focus on our breathing. Your breathing plays an incredibly important role in your stress levels. When you feel anxious, your breathing gets shallow, and when you are relaxed and calm, your breathing is deep and consistent (Princing, 2018). Using breathing as a method to recover from stress or to calm yourself when in a stressful situation is not a new idea; however, it is still very relevant. Your breathing can either induce panic or calm your nerves completely, depending on how you're breathing.

We touched on breathing techniques and the importance of breathing in Chapter 5, but in this chapter, we'll look at a bunch of different breathing techniques that can help you to regain your calm and put your nervous system at ease. Keep your journal nearby, and be sure to write down the techniques that you find interesting and would like to try first. If you try a technique and feel like it's not the one for you, don't hesitate to move on and try another as long as you don't give up on deep breathing altogether. Let's take a look at four of the most common breathing techniques in detail.

DEEP BREATHING TECHNIQUE

Deep breathing is a technique used to help with concentration, relaxation, and breathing out all things stressful. Follow the steps closely, and if you struggle with breathing in general, this might not be the best technique for you to start with (Rogel Cancer Center, 2014):

1. Sit down in a comfortable position. Let your arms hang relaxed, and make sure that you're not leaning over and covering your diaphragm.
2. Breathe deeply into the abdomen. This will release the shallow breathing in your upper chest and cause the lower abdomen to lower the stress response. As your diaphragm moves

downward, your stomach will move upward. Allow the air to go deeply into your abdomen.
3. Exhale as much as you can through your mouth. Become aware of your empty abdomen.
4. Inhale slowly through your nose and watch as your belly rises. Imagine the air filling your lungs deeply with fresh air and new life.
5. Exhale as completely as you can and repeat for 10 minutes.

AUTOGENIC RELAXATION

This technique uses verbal suggestions to promote physical relaxation. This method can also be considered meditation, where one moves away from distracting thoughts and focuses on something that encourages physical and mental relaxation (Rogel Cancer Center, 2014). This technique makes you aware of your body and brings you into the present:

- Repeat the following statement to yourself for 60 seconds: "My left hand is heavy. My left hand is heavy. I am at peace, and my left hand is heavy."
- Now, repeat the following statement to yourself for 60 seconds. "My right hand is heavy. My

right hand is heavy. I am at peace, and my right hand is heavy."

- Repeat the phrases, but substitute *hand* for foot, arm, leg, and your entire body.
- Repeat a couple of times a week.

PROGRESSIVE MUSCLE RELAXATION

The Progressive Muscle Relaxation technique focuses on specific parts of the body (Rogel Cancer Center, 2014). You will tense and relax your muscles in order to learn the difference between the sensations of tension and relaxation. If you constantly struggle with pain, this might not be the best method for you to start with (Rogel Cancer Center, 2014):

1. Start with your hands and clench your fists. Feel the tightness of your skin and hold in this position of discomfort for a couple of seconds. When it starts to get really uncomfortable, let go and notice the feeling of relaxation.
2. Now, repeat the same with your feet and toes. Flex your muscles and then release them after a couple of seconds.
3. Move on to all the other parts of your body, including your arms, legs, stomach, chest, and neck.

GUIDED IMAGERY RELAXATION

This technique focuses on detailed images, almost like a controlled daydream (Rogel Cancer Center, 2014). This helps the mind to switch off and reduce tension in the body:

1. Breathe deeply; inhale through your nose, and exhale through your mouth.
2. Imagine a scene that is appealing and relaxing to you. It can include anything from a walk in the park to laying on the beach. Make it personal to you and notice every detail of this *happy place*.
3. Think about what your image looks like, smells like, sounds like, feels like, and tastes like.
4. When you're ready to come back, slowly count back from ten before opening your eyes. Allow that calm to follow you back into reality.

OTHER

Besides the above techniques, there are many other breathing techniques that you can try. Below is a list with a short description of a couple of other techniques that you can use for relaxation and recovery. Feel free to do more research on the below methods and try a couple of different ones until you find one that you like.

Technique	Description
Breath Focus	Practice deep breathing (steps in Chapter 5), and while you are breathing deeply, picture something that makes you feel relaxed. As you breathe out, imagine pushing away all the negativity. Continue for 10 minutes.
Equal Breathing	Inhale and exhale in the same amount of time. Breathe in through your nose and count to five. Breathe out through your mouth and count to five as well. Continue for a couple of minutes. You can work up to 10 seconds of inhaling and exhaling.
Modified Lion's Breath	Imagine that you're a lion. Let all of your breath out by opening your mouth wide. Breathe in through your nose, and breathe out with a little roar or "HA" sound. Repeat several times.
Pursed Lip Breathing	This technique helps you keep your airway open for longer. Inhale slowly through your nostrils; purse your lips as if blowing something. Breathe out slowly through your pursed lips, taking twice as long as you did when you inhaled. Repeat a couple of times.
Diaphragmatic Breathing	Lie on your back and bend your knees. Place a pillow underneath your legs and put one hand on your chest and the other on your rib cage. Feel your diaphragm move. Inhale slowly and feel your stomach expand. Engage your stomach muscles to draw them toward the spine as you exhale. Keep your hands as still as possible.
Alternate Nostril Breathing	Sit comfortably, and place your left hand on your left knee and your right hand up towards your nose. Exhale completely, then use your right thumb to close the right nostril. Inhale through the left nostril, and then close the left nostril with your fingers. Open the right nostril and exhale through that side. Continue until the cycle is complete. Continue for five minutes.
Resonant Breathing	This technique allows you to breathe at a rate of five full breaths per minute. You achieve this by inhaling and exhaling for five counts. Inhale for five, exhale for five, and repeat for a few minutes.
Sitali Breathing	This technique lowers your body temperature and relaxes your mind. Stick your tongue out and curl the other edges together. You can purse your lips if your tongue can't keep that shape. Inhale through the mouth and exhale through the nose. Continue for five minutes.
Humming Bee Breathing	This technique provides you with instant calm. Close your eyes and relax your face. Place your first two fingers on the cartilage that partially covers your ear canal. Inhale, and gently press the fingers into the cartilage as you exhale. Keep your mouth closed and make a loud humming sound. Sit for a couple of minutes like this.

TECHNIQUE: DESCRIPTION

As you can see, there are a multitude of breathing exercises that you can try in order to recover and rest. All it requires is a little bit of input from you and putting away all distractions for a couple of minutes. Speaking of distractions, in the next chapter, we'll look at the digital world and how it contributes to stress. First, let's have a look at this chapter's journaling moment.

WRITE THE STRESS AWAY

For this chapter's journaling moment, I want you to redraw the following diagram in your journal to make it more personal, and then take 10 minutes to practice the deep breathing method you just drew.

Square Breathing

← Hold your breath for 4 seconds. ←		
↓ **Breathe out for 4 seconds.** ↓		↑ **Breathe in for 4 seconds.** ↑
→ Hold your breath for 4 seconds. →		

13

THE WOES OF TODAY'S WORLD

As we come to the end of this journey, there is one last topic that we need to talk about. Thousands of years ago, people were stressed by survival. Things like nature and hunting scared them, so why are we still stressed today even though we don't have to hunt or worry about hyper-thermia? Well, that's because we have modern woes causing us stress. The difference, however, is that thousands of years ago, stress led to survival, while now stress leads to more stress and an unenjoyable experience. In this chapter, I want to chat about the two most common modern-day woes: Remote work and social media.

We are currently using more technology than ever before. Almost no career choice comes without technology, and almost no relaxation method doesn't require technology. According to a study done in 2019, over 1.4 billion smartphones are shipped every year, and despite being beneficial in many areas, technology highly contributes to stress (Fischer et al., 2021).

Technology can cause stress in various ways, including (Harrison & Lucassen, 2019):

- Perpetual distraction caused by the flashing, beeping, and vibrations.
- Sleep dysregulation due to cell phones in bed before bedtime and as soon as one wakes up.
- An unbalanced work-life schedule due to work being remote.
- Fear of missing out due to social media showing you all the things you do not have.
- Social comparison and constant disinterest in reality.

Since the global pandemic, many people have moved from traditional workspaces to working remotely. As comfortable and adaptable as it is, it comes with the risk of added stress, which one should be aware of. However, with the correct tips, you can handle stress while enjoying the benefits of working remotely. Let's take a look at a couple of ways to handle the stress of remote work.

TIPS TO HANDLE THE STRESS OF REMOTE WORK

Prioritize Mental Health

When working remotely, calendars fill up quickly with meetings and deadlines, along with additional family responsibilities because you're home. Unfortunately, this means that we forget to prioritize mental health. You can protect your mental health by taking regular breaks and making use of time management. When you use a time management system, you schedule time for rest and don't just add it to the bottom of your list for when you're done with everything else. It also allows you to breathe for a couple of seconds and build a habit of gratitude (Wrike, 2022).

You Don't Have to Be Perfect

Many employees try to be perfect, especially when working from home, to prove that they're not slacking. According to a study, most people who work remotely feel pressure to prove their value to their employers (Wrike, 2022). Of course, it's wonderful that you want to work hard and deliver good work; however, don't try to hide your struggles in order to appear perfect. As soon as you're open about your struggles, you gain access to someone helping you. When you pretend to be perfect, you'll coop up stress and pretty soon be a ticking time bomb of burnout.

Create a Routine

One way that you can prevent stress when working remotely is to create a routine and stick to it. Good habits for working from home don't just appear magically; you need to work hard to put them in place. Having a routine strengthens your mental health, and it reduces the number of decisions that you need to make every day. You create more mental space to get things done when you stick to a routine (Wrike, 2022). Creating a routine will also help you to have *office hours*, preventing you from working from the moment you wake up to the moment you go to bed.

Track Your Work

When working remotely, it can be difficult to show the rest of your team what you've done. Many remote workers feel scared that they might be seen as less hardworking when they work remotely. One way to eliminate this stress is by tracking your progress transparently. Track the projects that you're busy with and when they're completed by keeping your colleagues in the loop and being honest when you haven't done something yet. Remove the pressure of *doing everything* by delegating to others and involving others in work (Wrike, 2022).

Say "No"

Unfortunately, many employers start pushing the boundaries when their employees work remotely. Work hours become longer, online meetings become more time-consuming, and more work gets handed out because they think you're at home and don't have to commute to work. Make sure you know what your contract states regarding working remotely, work hours, and expectations and find the courage to say no when something is expected of you that shouldn't be. Protecting your boundaries is the best way to protect your mental health and reduce stress.

Now that we've covered the different techniques for dealing with stress when working remotely, it's time to address the other culprit: technology.

ARE YOU STRESSED BY TECHNOLOGY?

Technology is a modern stressor that many overlook. However, technology can add a lot of stress to your life, despite being a wonderful invention (Strategic Psychology, 2015). The questionnaire below will help you to discover whether your stress levels are influenced by technology or not. Answer the questions truthfully in order to really assess whether technology is having a negative impact on your stress.

Question	Yes	No
Do you feel like you're juggling too much?		
Is your sleep impacted by technology?		
Do you feel like you spend too much time on social media?		
Are you constantly on your phone, computer, or TV?		
Are you so busy that you skip lunch?		
Do you drive everywhere to save time?		
Do you feel over-committed to the point that you have no time for yourself?		
TOTAL:		

If you answered "yes" to more than three of the above questions, chances are that you are in dangerous territory and highly affected by technology. In order to change that, you need to start managing digital stress.

MANAGING DIGITAL STRESS

If you got a high score in the previous exercise, it's time to manage your digital stress. Here are a few simple yet highly effective ways in which you can manage your digital stress a little better:

- Switch off from work at a dedicated time and mark yourself as offline.
- Put the phone away while you work.
- Turn off your notifications to prevent distractions.
- Have important conversations face-to-face, not over the phone.
- Be selective with your contacts, and don't allow everyone to have your number.
- Don't feel pressured to have all the apps and be active on all platforms.
- Do a digital detox and take a couple of weeks away from social media.
- Turn off all your gadgets before you go to bed at night to ensure peace and quiet.

WRITE THE STRESS AWAY

For today's journaling section, I want you to take time and meditate on the following question. Then set a timer for ten minutes and make a list of things that you can do to relax that don't involve technology. Try to add as many things as possible to the list. Then, choose one activity that you will do today to relax instead of watching TV or scrolling through social media. Before you do, here are a few questions to get your mind going:

1. When do I feel most relaxed?
2. What do I feel when I'm outdoors?
3. What do I feel when I spend a lot of time on social media?

CONCLUSION

And just like that, we've come to the end of our journey. However, this is only the end of our journey together, not the end of your stressed-out journey. In fact, your journey is only beginning now. My goal on this journey was to take your hand and equip you with all the tools and knowledge that you need to live a stress-free life, while your part of the journey is to now take those tools and make them your own.

We've come a long way, and together we have discovered a lot:

- You've learned that by turning back the pages and discovering the root of the stress, you can find the reason for your stress and take action against it.

- You've been equipped with the right tools to put out the flames and are aware of the dangers of burnout.
- Together, we discovered the true meaning of stress and the effect it has on our bodies.
- You have a clear understanding now of what triggers your stress and how to remove those triggers from your life.
- We've talked about overthinking and how we can free ourselves from the trap.
- You know now that you need to keep an eye on time management and how good management and organization can lead to a life with less stress.
- You are equipped with tools and tricks to find instant Zen, no matter the chaos you are facing.
- You have the ability and the power to transform your thoughts and practice positive self-talk daily.
- You understand the importance of emotion regulation, and you have the correct tools to regulate your own emotions in a way that is healthy.
- You understand self-care, and you know how to implement it.

- You've discovered the balance between rest and movement and the impact it has on your mind and body.
- You have all the breathing techniques you need to start on a journey of no stress.
- You understand what the modern-day culprits are and why social media can lead to stress.

As you can see, you've learned a lot and come a long way! I have full confidence and faith that you will take all of these tools and tricks and make the most of them. If there's one thing that you should remember, it's that this is not an overnight journey. But step-by-step, you'll start to feel the difference, and pretty soon, those around you will see the difference in you. My life would have looked very different if I had equipped myself with these tools and tricks sooner, but now I am happy to announce that I am no longer a slave to fear and stress, and I can't wait to hear about your success story either. Remember, you have the power to overcome the mental roadblocks that are in your way. By de-stressing yourself, you will uncover a whole new you—one that is filled with joy, peace, and excitement.

If this book has helped you in any way and you are now confident in your ability to manage your stress, please leave a review and share this knowledge with someone else who will also benefit from it. Let's reclaim our nature as one that is not stressed, one person at a time. Even though I have to say goodbye now, I know that you will find your Zen sooner rather than later.

PASS IT ON!

Now that you have all the tools and techniques you need to set yourself on a calmer and less stressed-out trajectory, you're in the perfect position to help someone else.

Simply by leaving your honest opinion of this book on Amazon, you'll show new readers where they can find the guidance they're looking for as they embark on their own journeys.

Thank you for your support. Together, we can build a future with less stress.

Scan the QR code below for a quick review!

REFERENCES

Ackerman, C. (2019, June 21). *What is self-regulation? (+95 skills and strategies).* PositivePsychology.com. https://positivepsychology.com/self-regulation/

Ackerman, C. (2021, December 6). *What is Self-Awareness and Why is it Important? [+5 Ways to Increase It].* PositivePsychology.com. https://positivepsychology.com/self-awareness-matters-how-you-can-be-more-self-aware/

Acosta, K. (2022, January 11). *What Causes Overthinking—And 6 Ways To Stop.* Forbes Health. https://www.forbes.com/health/mind/what-causes-overthinking-and-6-ways-to-stop/

Andrews, A. (2022). *How Can Time Management Help to Reduce Stress?* Zandax. https://www.zandax.com/blog/how-can-time-manage ment-help-reduce-stress

Avoiding Stress & Burnout when Working from Home Remote Work Guide. (2022). Wrike. https://www.wrike.com/remote-work-guide/remote-work-burnout-mental-health/

Ayres, M., & Vivyan, C. (2019). *The decider skills for self help : CBT and DBT skills to increase resilience, coping and confidence.* Michelle Ayres & Carol Vivyan.

Belle, L. (2021, May 18). No one is useless in this world who lightens the burdens of another. ~Charles Dickens. Medium. https://medium.com/the-daily-cuppa/no-one-is-useless-in-this-world-who-lightens-the-burdens-of-another-charles-dickens-a8bb7f06c13c

Black, M. (2022). *20 quotes for when you feel stressed.* Canva. https://www.canva.com/learn/inspiring-quotes-for-stress/

Blackman, A. (2018, August 11). *What are self-limiting beliefs? How to overcome them successfully.* Business Envato Tuts+. https://business.tutsplus.com/tutorials/what-are-self-limiting-beliefs--cms-31607

Cameron, D. (2022, March 15). *StackPath.* Contracting Business. https://www.contractingbusiness.com/contracting-business-success/article/21236195/5-steps-to-overcome-adversity-and-its-accompanying-uncertainty

Chowdhury, M. R. (2019, August 13). *What is emotion regulation? 6 emotional skills and strategies.* Positive Psychology. https://positivepsychology.com/emotion-regulation/

Common Stress Reactions - A Self-Assessment. (2000). Office of Mental Health.https://omh.ny.gov/omhweb/disaster_resources/pandemic_influenza/doctors_nurses/common_stress_reactions.html

Cuncic, A. (2022, January 27). *How to develop and use self-regulation in your life.* Verywell Mind. https://www.verywellmind.com/how-you-can-practice-self-regulation-4163536

Causes of stress. (2017, November). Mind. https://www.mind.org.uk/information-support/types-of-mental-health-problems/stress/causes-of-stress/

Daltrey, D. (2016, July 27). *What is overthinking - and what can we do about it?* Great Minds Clinic Blog. https://www.greatmindsclinic.co.uk/blog/what-is-overthinking-and-what-can-we-do-about-it/

Dysfunctional Beliefs Affecting Stress. (n.d.). MentalHelp. https://www.mentalhelp.net/stress/dysfunctional-beliefs-affecting-stress/

Elizabeth Scott. (2019). *What Are the Main Causes of Stress?* Verywell Mind. https://www.verywellmind.com/what-are-the-main-causes-of-stress-3145063

Elmer, J. (2022, January 25). *Drawing Therapy Techniques to Relieve Stress.* Psych Central. https://psychcentral.com/stress/art-therapy-ways-to-draw-your-stress-out#how-to

Estrada, J. (2020, October 25). *6 Ways to Practice Positive Self-Talk To Improve Self Esteem.* Well+Good. https://www.wellandgood.com/positive-self-talk/

Fischer, T., Reuter, M., & Riedl, R. (2021). *The Digital Stressors Scale: Development and Validation of a New Survey Instrument to Measure Digital Stress Perceptions in the Workplace Context.* Frontiers in Psychology. https://doi.org/https://doi.org/10.3389/fpsyg.2021.607598

Friedman, W. (2015). *Types of Stress and Their Symptoms - Dealing with Stress and Anxiety Management.* Coping Mechanisms from Mental Help. https://www.mentalhelp.net/blogs/types-of-stress-and-their-symptoms/

Facts & statistics. (2021, April 21). Anxiety and Depression Association of America. https://adaa.org/understanding-anxiety/facts-statistics

Five Fs: fight, flight, freeze, flop and friend. (n.d.). Rape Crisis England & Wales. https://rapecrisis.org.uk/get-help/tools-for-victims-and-survivors/understanding-your-response/fight-or-flight/

Goalbook Toolkit. (2022). Goal Book App. https://goalbookapp.com/toolkit/v/strategy/6-second-pause

Griffin, M. R. (2010, May 11). *10 Health Problems Related to Stress That You Can Fix.* WebMD. https://www.webmd.com/balance/stress-management/features/10-fixable-stress-related-health-problems

Harrison, G., & Lucassen, M. (2019, March 1). *Stress and anxiety in the digital age: the dark side of technology.* https://www.open.edu/openlearn/health-sports-psychology/mental-health/stress-and-anxiety-the-digital-age-the-dark-side-technology

Hundred and One Planners. (2021, November 9). *How to Overcome Limiting Beliefs with Free Printable Workbook.* 101 Planners. https://www.101planners.com/limiting-beliefs/

How Technology Can Increase Stress Levels. (2015, May 6). Strategic Psychology Canberra. https://strategicpsychology.com.au/why-are-we-so-stressed-the-tech-factor/

Helpful vs Harmful: Ways to Manage Emotions. (2019). Mental Health America. https://www.mhanational.org/helpful-vs-harmful-ways-manage-emotions

Invah. (2015, May 27). *10 Essential Emotion Regulation Skills for Adults.* Reddit. https://www.reddit.com/r/AbuseInterrupted/comments/37gtkv/10_essential_emotion_regulation_skills_for_adults/

Importance of stress awareness. (2020, April 1). Ieso Health. https://www.iesohealth.com/wellbeing-blog/the-importance-of-stress-awareness

Lawler, M. (2021, May 19). *What is self-care and why is it critical for your health?* Everyday Health. https://www.everydayhealth.com/self-care/

Lawson, K. (2016). *Become Aware of Your Stressors and Reactions.* Taking Charge of Your Health & Wellbeing. https://www.takingcharge.csh.umn.edu/become-aware-your-stressors-and-reactions

Levendusky, P. (2022, April 23). *Do You Manage Your Time Well?* McLean Hospital. https://www.mcleanhospital.org/essential/do-you-manage-your-time-well

Lindberg, S., & Weiss, K. (2022, July 14). *How to Calm Down: 22 Things to Do When You're Anxious or Angry.* Healthline. https://www.healthline.com/health/how-to-calm-down#tips-to-calm-down

Livingston, M. (2022, October 30). *Naturally Reduce Stress With These 8 Anxiety-Fighting Exercises.* CNET. https://www.cnet.com/health/fitness/naturally-reduce-stress-with-these-8-anxiety-fighting-exercises/

Lukowski, A. (2019). *Identifying Stressors.* National Jewish Health. https://www.nationaljewish.org/conditions/health-information/stress-and-relaxation/stress/stressors

Manson, M. (2018, May 3). *The Three Levels of...* Mark Manson. https://markmanson.net/self-awareness

Mawer, R. (2020, February 28). *17 Proven Tips to Sleep Better at Night.* Healthline. https://www.healthline.com/nutrition/17-tips-to-sleep-better#13.-Take-a-relaxing-bath-or-shower

Neff, K. (2011, April 17). *Is it self-indulgent to be self-compassionate?* Self-Compassion. https://self-compassion.org/is-it-self-indulgent-to-be-self-compassionate/

Neff, K. (2015, September 30). *The five myths of self-compassion.* Greater Good. https://greatergood.berkeley.edu/article/item/the_five_myths_of_self_compassion

Princing, M. (2018, June 4). *What Is Deep Breathing?* UW Medicine. https://rightasrain.uwmedicine.org/mind/stress/why-deep-breathing-makes-you-feel-so-chill#:~:text=Deep%20breathing%20can%20help%20lessen

Rizzo, A. (2021, November 22). *Self in IFS Therapy - what it is, what are the 8 C's and the 5 P's of Self.* Therapy with Alessio. https://www.therapywithalessio.com/articles/self-in-ifs-therapy-what-it-is-what-are-the-8-cs-and-the-5-ps-of-self

Robinson, L., & Smith, M. (2020, April 1). *Dealing with Uncertainty During the Coronavirus Pandemic.* HelpGuide. Https://Www.helpguide.org. https://www.helpguide.org/articles/anxiety/dealing-with-uncertainty.htm

Rogel Cancer Center. (2014, February 21). *Learning to Relax.* Rogel Cancer Center. University of Michigan. https://www.rogelcancercenter.org/breaking-habits-beating-us/learning-relax

Sachdev, P. (2021, June 22). *What Is Emotional Dysregulation?* WebMD. https://www.webmd.com/mental-health/what-is-emotional-dysregulation#:~:text=Emotional%20dysregulation%20is%20a%20term

Schultz, K. (2019, April 18). What is spoon theory? Healthline. https://www.healthline.com/health/spoon-theory-chronic-illness-explained-like-never-before#1

Scott, E. (2020, October 21). *How Your Personality Traits Can Put You at Risk for Burnout.* Verywell Mind. https://www.verywellmind.com/mental-burnout-personality-traits-3144514

Scott, E. (2022, May 24). *The Toxic Effects of Negative Self-Talk.* Verywell Mind. https://www.verywellmind.com/negative-self-talk-and-how-it-affects-us-4161304

Shah, N. (2016, February 2). *Why is time management key?* The Stress Management Society. https://www.stress.org.uk/why-is-time-management-key/

Smith, M., Segal, J., & Robinson, L. (2018, December 27). *Burnout prevention and treatment.* HelpGuide. https://www.helpguide.org/articles/stress/burnout-prevention-and-recovery.htm

Sprankles, J. (2021, August 5). *Feeling Burnt Out? Read These Quotes When You Need A Mental Reset.* Scary Mommy. https://www.scarymommy.com/burnout-quotes

Stress - How Sleep Can Affect Stress Levels. (2019, February 28). Banner Health. https://www.bannerhealth.com/healthcareblog/teach-me/how-sleep-can-affect-stress#:~:text=Lessens%20anxiety&text=It%20can%20overwork%20the%20heart

Stress. (2018). CAMH. https://www.camh.ca/en/health-info/mental-illness-and-addiction-index/stress

Stressors. (2019). Centre for studies on human stress. https://humanstress.ca/stress/what-is-stress/stressors/

Ten Self-Care Tips to Practice at Home to Relieve Stress. (2020, March 30). Triangle Family Dental Spa. https://www.trianglefamilydental.com/10-self-care-tips-for-a-stressful-time/

Top 10 Causes Of Stress And How To Beat Them. (2018). Realbuzz. https://www.realbuzz.com/articles-interests/health/article/top-10-causes-of-stress-and-how-to-beat-them/

Valcour, M. (2016, November). *4 Steps to Beating Burnout.* Harvard Business Review. https://hbr.org/2016/11/beating-burnout

Whittleton, L. (2018, August 16). *Developing self-awareness to manage stress.* Linkedin. https://www.linkedin.com/pulse/developing-self-awareness-manage-stress-lisa-whittleton/

Wignall, N. (2021, February 17). *7 Psychological Reasons You Overthink Everything.* Nick Wignall. https://nickwignall.com/7-psychological-reasons-you-overthink-everything/

Why does organizing help with anxiety? (2021, December 27). SAFETY4SEA. https://safety4sea.com/cm-why-does-organizing-help-with-anxiety/

What Is Stress? Symptoms, Signs & More. (2021, January 28). Cleveland Clinic. https://my.clevelandclinic.org/health/articles/11874-stress